Edward L. Walker is currently Professor of Psychology at the University of Michigan and holds a Research Career Award from the United States Public Health Service. He is author of numerous scientific articles which have appeared in professional periodicals since 1938.

Roger William Heyns was a teacher of psychology at the University of Michigan, where he became Dean of the College of Literature, Science, and the Arts and subsequently Vice President for Academic Affairs. He received the Distinguished Faculty Award from the University of Michigan in 1959. He became Chancellor of the Berkeley campus of the University of California in 1965. Chancellor Heyns' works include *The Psychology of Human Adjustment* (1958) and frequent contributions to psychological journals and books in psychology.

CONTEMPORARY TOPICS IN
PSYCHOLOGY SERIES

Edward L. Walker, Editor

Psychological Aspects of International Conflict
Ross Stagner, Wayne State University

An Anatomy for Conformity
Edward L. Walker,
The University of Michigan
and Roger W. Heyns,
University of California, Berkeley

Brooks/Cole Publishing Company,
Belmont, California

A Division of Wadsworth
Publishing Company, Inc.

An Anatomy for Conformity

An Anatomy
for Conformity

EDWARD L. WALKER
The University of Michigan

ROGER W. HEYNS
University of California, Berkeley

Brooks/Cole Publishing Company
Belmont, California

A Division of Wadsworth Publishing Company, Inc.

Brooks/Cole Publishing Company,
Belmont, California

A Division of Wadsworth Publishing
Company, Inc.

L. C. Cat. Card No.: 62-7525

Printed in the United States of America

PREFACE

Conformity is a persistent social problem. This book is an effort to show how analysis of this problem can lead to experimental research and how the conclusions from the research can yield general principles applicable to everyday problems.

Our approach was surprisingly simple. From general behavior theory we adopted a basic formula, which involved the concepts of *need, instrumental act,* and *goal.* When this formula — this anatomy — was applied to the problems of conformity and non-conformity, we were able to manipulate and control and, therefore, study and understand the conformist and non-conformist behavior.

The research was supported by a grant from the Ford Foundation. Time for the preparation of the first draft was made available through a sabbatical leave, which was granted by the Board of Regents of The University of Michigan.

E. L. W.

Ann Arbor, Michigan

This book grew out of The Ford Foundation Project on Conformity at The University of Michigan.

Project Participants:

John W. Atkinson	Horace M. Miner
Robert C. Birney	Patricia A. O'Connor
Harry A. Burdick	Alfred C. Raphelson
John S. Caylor	John A. Swets
Roger W. Heyns	Joseph Veroff
Wilbert J. McKeachie	Edward L. Walker

CONTENTS

To
Alice
and
Ester

An Anatomy for Conformity

1

CONFORMITY AS A SOCIAL

AND THEORETICAL PROBLEM

Current commentary on the state of American culture abounds in concern for the growth and development of conformity as an enduring and determining characteristic of our civilization. The uniformity in manner and dress in the adolescent is deplored. Feminine skirt hems and waistlines rise and fall in an epochal ballet with an annual cadence. State legislatures frequently entertain and sometimes pass legislation requiring teachers, university professors and state employees to swear periodically to their loyalty to God, the Constitution or to whatever the originator of the legislation considers currently unimpeachable.

As the problem grows in apparent importance, the tendency to describe it in evaluative terms rather than in objective ones also grows. "Pressure toward uniformity" becomes "pressure toward mediocrity." The "brilliant" man becomes the "egghead." "The age of the common man" becomes "the age of the boob."

The problems

The evaluative words removed, one can detect and delineate at least five different problems. It is immediately apparent that conformity *per se* is not necessarily bad. In some realms of behavior it is desirable and in others it is definitely not so. A second problem involves the degree of uniformity in behavior and thinking which is commendable. The authority setting the pattern toward which uniformity pressures are exerted constitutes a third problem. Fourth are the kind and classes of conditions which produce conformity. Fifth is the question of what kinds of people conform and what kinds do not when the situation permits a choice. Some of these questions might be subject to basic research procedures and some might not. Let us consider them briefly in turn.

A "free society" is not "free." It is one in which there is a delicate balance between self-determined activity on the part of its citizens and activity conforming to standards set by the society. A social pattern in which every individual is permitted to do exactly as he wishes in every respect is almost inconceivable and has probably never existed. Some early frontier societies in America may have come as close as any in modern times, but even Tombstone, Arizona had its code. The other extreme, a completely controlled human society or even a really severely controlled one has probably never existed outside of George Orwell's *1984*.

Examination of almost any society, either past or present, reveals that there are activities that are restricted, others where deviation is a matter of indifference, and still others where deviation and difference is encouraged or even required.

In our society criminal law constitutes one set of specifications regarding areas in which the activities of the individual are restricted and exact conformity to the standards is a goal. Many, if not most, laws prevent one individual from infringing on the rights and, therefore, the freedoms of other individuals. Thus, restrictions upon freedom are specified and enforced in the name of freedom.

Many areas of activity, however, have rather wide limits of permissible deviation from the norm or standard of society. American men wear neckties, but there are few situations in which the deviant non-wearer is penalized for his deviance. Whether one reads books, owns a television set, belongs to a minority church group are matters of no great concern to the society as a whole.

There are still other areas of activity, and important ones, in which non-conformity is rewarded, especially if the average or mean performance is taken as a standard. Instances even exist in which deviation of one kind is rewarded and deviation of another kind punished. The outstanding athlete can be a non-conformist without negative sanction. In the classroom, a specifiable norm is to pass, to do well enough to progress normally toward graduation. Here the rewards are usually multiplied for the outstanding student, while punishments are meted out to the non-conforming dolt. Since these patterns are repeated in many areas where rewards come largely as a result of conformity, where non-conformity is rewarded only in the "successful" person, where non-conformity is punished in the unsuccessful, habitually unsuccessful people are likely to be more conformist than habitually successful people.

In this context, then, the problem of conformity lies in its appearance in areas where it is inimical to the common good. Some Eastern universities are said to contain within their cultures the tradition of the "gentleman's C." Truly excellent work is held in low repute, and the truly outstanding student is disparagingly referred to as a "grind." Presumably the expulsion of communists from university faculties is no threat if they are banished for their membership in a foreign espionage organization. If, however, removal is largely based on the faculty member's holding a divergent and unpopular viewpoint, then conformity is being enforced in a dangerous area. Intellectual progress occurs through individual, novel insight. The occurrence of insight is itself a revolutionary process. If revolutionary thinking in politics is to be suppressed, it becomes difficult to encourage revolutionary thinking in the sciences, the humanities, and the arts. This is especially true when science and politics are inextricably intertwined, as they have recently become.

It is clear then that the optimum degree of uniformity in behavior and ways of thinking will vary with the area of behavior under consideration. Few would object to complete conformity to the Golden Rule. Complete conformity in art is a contradiction in terms. Thus no particular degree of conformity is inherently bad. How much is good and how much is bad is a value judgment which will depend on the time, the place, the culture, the behavior, and the person who is making the judgment.

Conformity must always be in reference to some norm or standard. The standard implied in the "gentleman's C" is the mean or modal performance of the group. Obedience or compliance involves avoidance of the extremes. Frequently the standard set by society is quite different from the mean performance. Our society attempts to achieve conformity to the standard of complete pre-marital chastity; yet if Dr. Kinsey's books can be accepted as evidence of modal behavior, there is a rather wide gap between society's standard and the mean performance. Effective leaders sometimes set standards and achieve a high degree of conformity to them, even when the standard is far from the normal behavior of the group. It is said that during the Cuban revolution led by Fidel Castro in 1959, Castro's followers remained completely abstinent with respect to alcohol at his behest. This level of sobriety is not ordinarily characteristic of a revolutionary army.

Thus the norm or standard to which a group conforms may originate from a single person or from a group of any size, including, as a limit, the total group. It may range from a coincidence with the typical performance of the group to behavior which is not only atypical of that group but may be outside the range of normal behavior for the group.

Sometimes the norm is such that general agreement calls it good: "Thou shalt not kill." Sometimes there would be consensus that the norm is bad. An example might be the requirement that a young buck take the head of an enemy before he is accepted as a man in some of the head-hunting tribes. More often than not, the goodness or badness of the norm depends on one's point of view.

Therefore, the three questions about *the area in which conformity should or should not occur, the degree of conformity, and the origin of the norm or standard* are usually value questions. Judgments of good and bad in reference to them can be expected to vary from person to person, from group to group, and from time to time. They are not questions open to solution through basic research. The two additional questions concerning *the kinds and classes of conditions which produce conformity* and *the kinds of people who do conform and the kinds who do not* may be attacked experimentally.

A conceptualized anatomy for conformity

Conformity is a class of behavior. As such it should be manipulatable like any other class of behavior. The simplest formula describing the way in which behavior is ordinarily manipulated is:

NEED——————→INSTRUMENTAL ACT——————→GOAL

If you are a good boy or girl, Santa Claus will bring presents. If you make an excellent grade record in school, you will receive a scholarship. If you work hard in a business organization, you will receive a promotion and an increase in salary. All of these statements imply some need and a closely relevant goal, with an instrumental act—being good, making good grades or working hard—standing between the individual and the achievement of the goal. Conformity and non-conformity are instrumental acts, means to ends, ways of achieving goals to satisfy needs.

What, then, distinguishes conformity or non-conformity from other classes of instrumental acts? Let us define conformity as movement toward some norm or standard and non-conformity as movement away from such a norm or standard. This definition implies a dimension of some kind which permits specification of at least three points: an original position for a person or group, a point or position specified as a norm, and a second position of the person or group somewhere on the continuum.

Let us assume a dimension on which there are a number of specifiable positions. We can then picture conformity and non-conformity as follows:

1	2	3	4	5
	↑	↑	↑	↑
	N-C ←————→ OP ←————→ C			N

N = Norm
N-C = Non-conformity, movement away
OP = Original position
C   = Conformity, movement toward

Conformity and non-conformity always involve movement or change. This is true even when only a single observation is possible and change is not directly observable. To describe a person or a group as conformist on the basis of a single observation implies an earlier state in which the degree of agreement with the norm was not so great.

A norm in this formulation can be any standard from any source. Social norms usually involve sanctions, either positive, negative or both, and some agency to administer them. In the formulation this characteristic of the norm will be handled within the framework of the need-goal relationship.

For present purposes, the definition of the need and goal may be very simple at the outset. A need can be said to be aroused by any set of cues or instructions which lead to activity, and a goal can be defined as any state or condition which, when achieved, produces a cessation of the aroused activity. Increasing the specificity of this definition offers numerous problems, some of which will be treated later.

Situational manipulation of conformity

If one wishes to produce conformity, it is only necessary to arouse a need or motive, proffer a goal which satisfies that need, and make conformity necessary to the achievement of that goal. All of the manipulations of situations to be recounted in later chapters involve changes in one or another aspect of this simple procedure. Let us consider briefly some of the possible variations of this formula.

The instrumental act is subject to almost infinite variation within the framework we have chosen. For example, conformity might be expected to vary with the clarity of the norm. It can be expected to vary with the relative ambiguity of the situation in which the subject finds himself. If the subject knows exactly what the norm is, then complete conformity is possible. If the subject is highly uncertain of the norm, within the limits of his uncertainty, conformity must be more or less a matter of chance. We are all familiar with the faux pas which results from lack of familiarity with the requirements of a sub-culture. The variety of unacceptable table manners to be observed in entering college freshmen and the "bad" manners of the tourist are both common examples of non-conformity attributable to lack of knowledge of what the normative behavior is.

On the other hand the norm is often quite clear, but the range of behaviors which will satisfy the norm is not. The boss must be satisfied, but what will satisfy the boss may be in considerable question. This is a matter of stimulus ambiguity. For example, in the matter of table manners, the freshman pledge to the fraternity who has come from a very different sub-culture may observe the actions of his elders and quickly conform to the norm. The changes will be made in a minimum length of time and with a minimum of false moves. The pattern provided by the upperclassmen will be, it is to be hoped, an unambiguous stimulus. In contrast, the same freshman taking his meals in cafeterias and restaurants is in a much more ambiguous situation with respect to proper table manners. The stimulus situation is ambiguous, and progress toward the manners of the larger cultural group can be expected to be slow and subject to numerous changes, not all of which will be in the "right" direction. This difference can be attributed to the relative ambiguity of the stimulus situation.

The source of the norm is undoubtedly an important determinant of the degree of conformity which it can command. Sources can vary in many ways. One way is the degree of identification that an individual feels with the source. Individuals usually feel more closely identified with their own family than with a vague group such as "other people." If a subject is a member of a fraternity, a norm attributed to another fraternity of equal status can be expected to have more weight than a norm attributed to "students of the University of Siwash."

With source of norm and relative ambiguity constant, the effectiveness of the norm can vary with the amount of information the subject possesses about the expertness of the norm source. If a subject has had much experience in the area in question, and a norm he knows to be in error is attributed to a fraternity, it may produce little conformity. Saying that the boys do not date girls who live in dormitories may not be effective if the subject knows by experience that fraternity boys do in fact date dormitory girls frequently.

In situations where the attitudes of the reference group is clear, conformity may be made to vary by either enhancing or depreciating the expertness of the group in question. If a norm is attributed to people in general, and the qualification is added that the group is seldom wrong, we may expect more influence than if the statement is qualified with the phrases that very few people know anything about the subject under consideration and there is thus no reason to expect the group as a whole to be right.

Conformity can be expected to vary with the subject's own expertness. If a subject feels that he is in a better position than the reference group to judge, then the attributed opinion of the reference group can have little effect. For example, a well-read Frenchman who has visited the United States might be less influenced by Soviet propaganda concerning the standard of living in the United States than his less well-read and less peripatetic provincial countryman. Experimental variations in this respect can be achieved easily by varying the target or object of the norm. Changes in attitude or behavior can be effected much more readily toward a group the subject knows little about than toward a group with which he is intimately acquainted.

Other things being equal, norms probably function in direct proportion to the need-goal relationships they serve. The greater the need, the greater the conformity. The larger the reward or punishment, the greater the conformity. In many important social situations it is the probability of reward or punishment which is the controlling factor. Non-conformity with respect to some social norm might be very likely if the probability of negative sanctions is very low. Criminal behavior is often partially explained in this manner. Automobile theft, for example, might be expected to occur very infrequently if detection and punishment were certain, and if that certainty were well-known to everyone. The exact functional relation between the perceived probabilities of detection and punishment and the effectiveness of the punishment is a fascinating problem and is undoubtedly quite complex; but the demonstration of two degrees of conformity with two degrees of probability of sanction should be quite simple.

Conformity and conflict

The variables we have discussed have been treated as if we were dealing with a single need, a single instrumental act, and a single goal. In most social situations this simplicity of need-goal structure does not prevail. More often than not the individual can be characterized as possessing a variety of needs, as having available to him a variety of instrumental acts which might satisfy a number of goals in various combinations and in various degrees. Most real life situations are characterized by conflict.

The simplest formulation of a conflict situation with respect to conformity is one in which the individual possesses two predominant needs: one, which can be satisfied by conformity to a norm or standard, and the other, which can be satisfied by non-conformity. The sexual conflict of the young unmarried is an example. Conformity to social and moral standards demands celibacy. The biological system demands gratification.

Of the conflicts between instrumental acts, some involve more stress than others. The need to be accepted by society at large may produce conflict over the mode of activity which will achieve it. A child in the early teens may be in conflict over achievement as a star athlete or as an outstanding student. The intensity of the conflict, therefor, is often a function of the degree to which these two avenues of achievement are incompatible.

More often than not conflict is a mixture of multiple needs, multiple instrumental acts, and multiple goals or standards. Thus the need to be accepted by an adolescent group that is bent on rejection of parental standards may be in conflict with the need to achieve status in society at large. We might distinguish a need for acceptance by others and, in conflict with that, a need to "achieve" in an abstract sense. The satisfaction of one need requires the breaking of a series of social rules, while the satisfaction of the other requires strict conformity to a set of rules. As is often the case this situation is less of a conflict between conformity and non-conformity in a simple sense, but more of a conflict between two sets of norms or standards which cannot be conformed to simultaneously. Conformity to the rebellious standards of the adolescent peer group involves non-conformity to the standards of the parent and the society at large which they represent. No study of conformity would be complete without the inclusion of some element of conflict.

Conformity as a characteristic of an individual

In a given situation it is frequently the case that some individuals will conform and others will not. It is a common belief that some individuals can be characterized as being conformists and others as non-conformists. In most instances this is probably a confusion in the analysis of the situation. The group of artists who lived in Greenwich Village in the Twenties were frequently referred to as non-conformists. It was implied that either through training or selection, these people had come to be persistent deviants from social norms. It might be better to look upon them as conformists rather than non-conformists. They established group identity, they developed bohemian norms within their own sub-culture, and conformity to these norms was slavish indeed. It is only when their behavior is viewed in terms of the norms of a broader society that they appear non-conformist. It may very well be that conformity or non-conformity as *characteristics* of an individual are rare and that most instances of either class of behavior can be explained in situational terms.

On the other hand, there are situations in which some individuals tend to conform and others do not, although the situation is essentially the same for everyone. Such differences in behavior in an identical situation must be attributed to differences in personality.

Personality theory, as a discipline, provides many ways of describing individual differences. It seems certain that a great number of the terms by which personalities are described could be related to conformity behavior. The simple basic formula of Need⟶ Instrumental Act⟶Goal has such a universal character that it can be incorporated in any suitable descriptive category of personality structure.

The formula or model creates immediate predispositions in approach to the problem of how an individual might come to be characterized as conformist or non-conformist. For example, the individual may have acquired a pattern of needs satisfied more often than not by apparent conformity. On the other hand, conforming behavior might develop into a general habit. Both possibilities might bear further explication.

The concept of acquired motives is general within psychology and the social sciences. If someone acquires a motive, he does so with respect to certain environmental cues, which become capable of arousing the motive in question. The Need⟶Instrumental Act⟶Goal formula does not specify any particular motive as uniquely associated with conformity. Therefore, theoretically at least, any motive may serve to activate conformity behavior.

Among a large variety of categories of discernible human needs, the need for Affiliation has been selected as one that might be conducive to conformity more frequently than many others. Conformity behavior is interpersonal in nature, and the need for Affiliation is intimately related to interpersonal behavior. These apparent associations lead to a testable proposition or set of propositions. If an individual has acquired high need for Affiliation, if in the process a wide variety of situations have acquired the capacity to arouse the motive, and if conformity has in the past often been instrumental in satisfying that need, then the individual might conform in a variety of situations in which a choice seems available. It would, however, be a need for Affiliation which would characterize the individual rather than be a trait of conformity.

This proposition seems more testable if the conditional clauses are separated and treated individually. Whatever the approach, however, it is initially necessary to develop a measuring instrument distinguishing degrees of need for Affiliation. In a situation where the need is aroused in some standard manner, and conformity is seen as instrumental to affiliation, the amount of conformity should vary with the amount of the need. In the same situation two or more degrees of arousal might be achieved with the expectation that the greater the arousal of the affiliative need, the greater the conformity in the group. A further variation would involve the simultaneous arousal of two needs and a situation in which conformity and non-conformity served one or the other of the aroused needs. If both needs are measured, predictions could be made on the basis of the differences in strength of the two needs.

That conformity as an instrumental act might become a habit independent of the need involved is also a possibility. As such it might be specific in a limited class of situations, or if it has proved to be instrumental in a wide variety of situations in the past, it might become a general habit. This characteristic of a person might be more difficult to assess, but it should not be difficult to set up a situation in which the individual has the opportunity to learn to conform in order to achieve a goal. Should this prove to be the case, additional tests could provide information as to the extent to which the newly acquired habit tends to generalize.

An anatomy for conformity

This, then, is the simple anatomy for conformity. Whenever conforming behavior stands between a need of the individual and his achievement of a goal which will satisfy that need, conforming behavior will tend to occur. This book is a simple expansion of this basic framework.

2

STIMULUS AMBIGUITY

AS A FACTOR IN CONFORMITY

The primary variable to be considered in this chapter is the relative ambiguity of the stimulus situation in which an individual finds himself, and the effect of the ambiguity of a situation on conforming behavior. A single point of light in a dark room is seen to wander seemingly at random. This apparent movement is called the autokinetic effect. Because of the extreme ambiguity of a pin point of light in a dark room as a stimulus, it should be easy to influence a person to conform to some perceived (supposed) norm or standard. Conforming behavior should be easy to obtain. On the other hand, if one is presented with a line of standard length along with a set of lines which vary in size and among which only one is the same length as the standard, one has a highly structured stimulus situation. If a person is asked to find a line equal in length to the standard, and an attempt is then made to influence his choice in the direction of an obviously false selection simply because it is the apparent choice of a large group of people, then conformity should be relatively difficult to obtain. This would be true because of the highly structured nature and the lack of ambiguity of the stimulus. Unfortunately, it is difficult to measure the difference in ambiguity of the stimuli in the two situations independently of their effects on conformity.[1]

Stimulus ambiguity in a social situation may be defined in many ways. One way is to present a problem situation and ask how many alternate solutions seem appropriate. If only one solution is offered, we have a minimum of social stimulus ambiguity. If the answer is that any one of eight or ten alternates might be appropriate, then the situation can be described as more ambiguous. In a social situation with minimum stimulus ambiguity, conformity in response to some attempt to influence the opinion or behavior of a person should be relatively small. With a social situation of maximum stimulus ambiguity, conformity should be considerably greater.

Furthermore, individuals could be expected to differ in how ambiguous a social situation appears to them, depending on their past experience in general and their particular experiences with similar situations—in short, depending on their own personality. A person who sees a given social situation as highly ambiguous should be easier to influence or to be made to conform than a person who sees the situation as unambiguous.

The degree of conformity should vary with the likelihood that sanctions will be imposed for non-conformity. It seems a patent observation that the behavior of an individual in private might be considerably less conforming to social standards than it is in public. Furthermore, the nature of the difference can be expected to vary with the group that is to observe the behavior and thus be in a position to apply sanctions. Ideally, an experiment in this area would attempt to create a situation in which an individual is permitted to carry out behavior relevant to some norm or standard in private (except for an unsuspected observer) and then be induced to perform the same behavior in public. The behavior could be something as simple as the table manners of a teenager when alone, as opposed to his table manners when dining out with his parents.[2]

It is considerably simpler and possibly as useful to ask a person what he would do in a given situation if no one were to find out about it, ask him what he thinks a given group would expect, and then ask what he would do if he were certain that the group would find out what he had done. If there is a discrepancy between what he says he would do if unobserved, and what he thinks the group would expect, there is the possibility of conforming behavior. If his behavior in private is farther from the norm than his public behavior, then, by definition, conforming behavior can be said to have occurred.

An Experiment

An experiment which involves the relation of stimulus ambiguity to the degree of conforming behavior has a set of minimum requirements.

(1) It is necessary to create situations that involve more than one degree of stimulus ambiguity, and if possible, situations seen as involving different degrees of stimulus ambiguity by different people.

(2) It is necessary to obtain an opinion or attitude of people in a standard situation and then to elicit opinions on the same subject under conditions involving social pressure.

(3) Finally, it is necessary to develop quantitative measures of the extent of conforming behavior under social pressure and quantitative measures of stimulus ambiguity.

The experimental situation

Such a situation was created by developing a questionnaire similar to one used by Stouffer in a study of conflict of roles.[3] In the questionnaire developed for this purpose a subject was asked to reveal his attitudes toward a student proctor's responsibilities in dealing with the problem of cheating on a course examination. Each was presented with the following situation:

> Consider the general case of a student proctor who sees a fellow student cheating on the examination in some large introductory level course. Assume that the proctor does not know the student who is cheating.

In order to permit assessment of individual differences in the stimulus ambiguity of the situation, as well as different degrees of stimulus ambiguity between situations, each person was also given the following instructions:

Indicate your degree of approval of each of these interpretations of the proctor's job, as you see it, by the number of points you assign for each interpretation. In answering, you may assign any number of approval points from 0 to 100 to any one of the interpretations, but the total must equal exactly 100. Be sure to assign some number to each interpretation even if that number is 0.

Interpretation

———— In almost all cases report him for cheating.
———— In a substantial majority of the cases report him for cheating.
———— In a slight majority of the cases report him for cheating.
———— In a slight majority of the cases NOT report him for cheating.
———— In a substantial majority of the cases NOT report him for cheating.
———— In almost all cases NOT report him for cheating.

A subject's *private attitude* was then obtained by asking the following question:

If you didn't have to answer to anyone for your decision, if you were setting policy for the entire college (students, faculty, deans), how would you interpret the proctor's responsibilities? Make a first and second choice.

The next step was to see what happened to this expressed opinion when social pressure was applied first in one direction and then the other. First, the subject was asked how the student body would expect the proctor to behave in this problem setting. The answer given could be called the subject's *perception of the student norm*. He was then asked about his hypothetical behavior in the situation in which the students were bound to know of his action, although the college authorities would remain ignorant of them unless the subject himself reported the cheater to the authorities. This value was called the *student public attitude*. It was expected that many subjects would expect the student norm to be more lenient than their own position, and that the certainty that the students would know of their action would produce pressure toward conformity to the student norm.

Finally, the subjects were asked how the college authorities would expect the proctor to act in the general problem setting. His answer provided his *perception of the authority norm*. His answer to how he would act in the situation if the authorities were bound to know of his actions, whatever they might be, although the students would be very unlikely to ever hear of it, yielded his *authority public attitude*. It was anticipated that a subject would see the college authorities as more punitive than the subject himself, and thus the *authority public attitude* might reflect conforming behavior toward the *authority norm*.

The whole process described above was repeated by having the subjects again distribute their probabilities and make the five choices in the same situation, with different instructions:

> But this time assume that the student whom the proctor sees cheating is his own roommate and close friend. The roommate is a hard-working though not a brilliant student and desperately needs a good grade in this course.

Thus the two situations presented to the subjects might be described as the case of the *Unknown Student* and the case of the *Roommate Friend*. It was hoped that these two situations might differ in stimulus ambiguity and thus produce different degrees of conformity.

The measure of conformity

Since in each instance the subjects were asked for a first and second choice, it is possible to convert the six-point scale (the six choices listed on page 15) into a ten-point scale and plot each subject's choices for each of the problems as illustrated for a hypothetical subject in Figure 1.

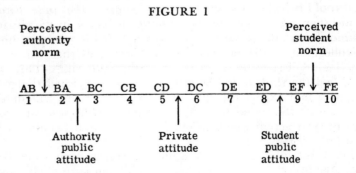

FIGURE 1

For conformity to occur, it is first necessary that there be a discrepancy between the *private attitude* and the *perceived norm*. In the hypothetical instance illustrated in the figure there is a large discrepancy in each direction. Furthermore, this hypothetical subject conformed to the *perceived authority norm* when it was certain that whatever he did would become known to the authorities. His *authority public attitude* is considerably more punitive than his *private attitude.* Similarly, his *student public attitude* is considerably more lenient than his *private attitude.*

A simple index of conforming behavior is as follows: If all five points in Figure 1 coincide, a score of zero is assigned. For each discrepancy between the *private attitude* and a *perceived norm,* a point is assigned. For each instance of movement toward a *perceived norm* an additional point is assigned. Thus with respect to each problem, that of the case of the unknown student and that of the case of the roommate friend, it is possible for an individual to achieve a conformity score ranging from zero to four.

The measure of stimulus ambiguity

When subjects were asked to assign 100 approval points among a set of alternative behaviors as indicated on page 15, they were really induced to express the amount of uncertainty they felt concerning the appropriate action of the proctor. If a subject assigns all of his points to one alternative, it is clear that for this subject there is no uncertainty in the situation. If a subject distributes the 100 approval points evenly between the alternatives, he is indicating a maximum of uncertainty with respect to the appropriate behavior on the part of the proctor.

A quantitative measure of the amount of uncertainty in any pattern of distribution of approval points is provided by a measure of uncertainty developed by Shannon in his classic work on information theory.[4] In the general case the function is described by the formula:

$$U = -\Sigma \, p_i(\log_2 p_i), \text{ where}$$
$$U = \text{uncertainty}$$
$$p_i = \text{probability of occurrence of the Ith response}$$
$$\Sigma p_i = 1.00$$

If we apply this formula for uncertainty to the distribution of p_i's provided by each subject (the subject's distribution of the 100 approval points), we can obtain an *index of stimulus ambiguity* which expresses ambiguity in terms of the information theory unit of bits. The number of bits is defined as the log to the base 2 of the number of equiprobable responses available to be made to a signal or stimulus.

TABLE 1

EXAMPLE OF RESPONSE DISTRIBUTIONS AND

ASSOCIATED AMBIGUITY INDEX VALUES

Subject	Responses							Ambiguity
	A	B	C	D	E	F	G	index × 100
Jon	0	100	0	0	0	0	0	0
Jan	0	80	20	0	0	0	0	72
Joe	0	0	0	50	50	0	0	100
Jen	0	0	0	0	33	34	33	158
Jud	14	14	14	16	14	14	14	281

Table 1 illustrates the application of this formula to the responses of five hypothetical subjects to a situation in which there are seven alternatives. It can thus be seen that if there is no ambiguity in the situation, if all approval points are assigned to one alternative as in the case of Jon, the ambiguity index will have a zero value. If the situation is highly ambiguous as in the case of Jud, the stimulus ambiguity index will have a maximum value, in this instance in the vicinity of 280.

The experimental subjects

Originally there were one hundred twenty-three subjects in the study. They were volunteers recruited from four sociology classes at what was then Michigan State Normal College but which is now Eastern Michigan University. They were predominantly women in the junior and senior classes. Incomplete responses, failure to follow instructions, and internally inconsistent responses (selection of an alternative outside the range of their own designated set of possible interpretations) reduced the number of useable protocols to numbers ranging from 81 to 117 depending on the analysis to be made. The results of the analyses of the two problems follow.

Stimulus ambiguity and conformity

The general proposition states that the more ambiguous a stimulus situation, the more the possibility of movement; and the more the possibility of movement, the more the likelihood of conformity as a function of social pressure. This proposition can be tested if

FIGURE 2

CONFORMITY AND STIMULUS AMBIGUITY

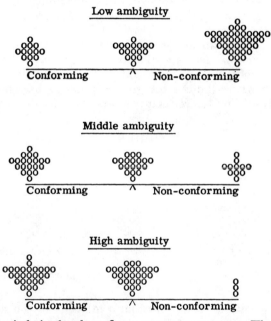

Each circle in the above figure represents a person. The upper figure represents the behavior of subjects with relatively low ambiguity indices (0-100). It shows that the majority had low conformity scores (0-1). A smaller number had middle conformity scores (2), while an even smaller number had high conformity scores (3-4). The middle figure illustrates the conformity behavior of subjects with middle indices of stimulus ambiguity (101-150), and the lower figure illustrates the conformity behavior of subjects with high stimulus ambiguity scores (151-up).

the individual subjects differ widely with respect to the extent that they see a situation as clear or ambiguous. There are quite large individual differences in the relative ambiguity of the proctor's duties as seen by the subjects in this experiment. Therefore the general proposition can be tested by making a comparison between the stimulus ambiguity indices and the conformity indices. Such a comparison may be seen in Figure 2.

When subjects see the situation as relatively unambiguous, thus having low ambiguity, the number of conformers is small. As the ambiguity of the stimulus situation increases to a middle level and then to a high level (very ambiguous), the number of conforming subjects increases markedly.[5] *The finding is the greater the stimulus ambiguity, the greater the likelihood of conformity.*

The same point can be demonstrated if the two situations, that of the *Unknown Student* and that of the *Roommate Friend*, differ in stimulus ambiguity. Greater conformity would be expected in the situation where there is the greater stimulus ambiguity. Figure 3 compares the stimulus ambiguity scores made by the same subjects

FIGURE 3

DIFFERENCES IN THE RELATIVE STIMULUS AMBIGUITY
OF THE TWO SOCIAL SITUATIONS

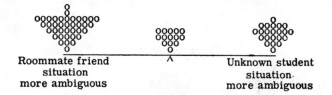

Roommate friend	Unknown student
situation	situation
more ambiguous	more ambiguous

in the two situations. It is clear that a majority of the subjects saw the case of the roommate friend as the more ambiguous. Therefore, more conformity can be expected in this case than in the case of the unknown student. The results of this comparison may be seen in Figure 4.

It seems clear from an examination of the two figures that with other things equal, *the greater the ambiguity of a situation, the greater the amount of conformity which can be expected to occur.* At least this seems to be true in a comparison of two situations which differ slightly in relative stimulus ambiguity.

FIGURE 4

DIFFERENCES IN THE FREQUENCY OF CONFORMITY IN THE TWO SOCIAL SITUATIONS

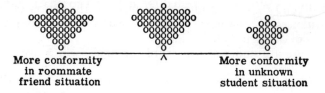

More conformity
in roommate
friend situation

∧

More conformity
in unknown
student situation

Public versus private behavior and conformity

There are several findings of interest obtained in this study which are illustrated in Figure 5. The figure illustrates the mean privately held attitude in each case with the middle figure. In each

FIGURE 5

PUBLIC VERSUS PRIVATE BEHAVIOR AND CONFORMITY

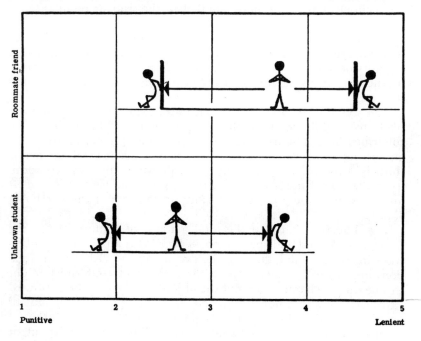

Roommate friend

Unknown student

1   2   3   4   5

Punitive   Lenient

case the figure pushed toward the punitive end of the scale represents the attitude expressed if the authorities are certain to learn of the action taken, while the small figure pushed to the right toward the more lenient end of the scale represents the response to the likelihood that the students will learn of the action taken. The four instances of movement along the scale represent four different instances of conformity behavior.[6]

There are a number of aspects of the figure which are worthy of note:

In general students tend to choose positions on the punitive end of the scale. It will be remembered that the original scale was ten units in length (see page 16) with the higher scores representing lenient attitudes. All mean scores in the figure are so well contained within the punitive end that the lenient end of the scale was not drawn in the figure.

As might be expected the students tend to see the authorities as holding a more punitive attitude toward cheating, but it was a surprise to find that most individual students see students in general as holding much more lenient attitudes. Thus individual students see themselves as being more moral than the student population as a whole.

As might be expected, students tend to have attitudes which are somewhat more punitive toward an *Unknown Student* than toward a hard working and deserving *Roommate Friend*. Yet the behavior of cheating is by no means condoned even under these circumstances.

The well-known finding that attitudes expressed in private are likely to be different than those expressed in public is clearly reconfirmed here. The possibility that either the students alone or the authorities alone would learn of the action taken produces major shifts in attitude. The *authority norm* produces the more conformity in the case of the *Roommate Friend,* while the *perceived student norm* produces the greater conformity in the case of the *Unknown Student.*

The difference between the total amount of conformity for the *Roommate Friend* and the *Unknown Student* is attributed to differences in stimulus ambiguity in the two situations. Other interpretations are possible. Differences in the amount of conformity might also be due to characteristics of the object or target of the expressed attitude. While it is not so apparent from Figure 5, the amount of conformity is slightly greater in response to the *perceived authority norm* than to the *perceived student norm.* Thus conformity might also be expected to vary with characteristics of the source of the norm. This aspect of conformity constitutes the subject of the next chapter.

Summary

Conformity behavior can be expected to vary as a function of the degree of stimulus ambiguity in a social situation as it is seen by a given person. If he sees the situation as one in which the alternative behaviors open to him are few in number and well-defined, social pressure is unlikely to produce much change in his attitudes. If, however, he sees the situation as permitting many alternative behaviors, and if he is uncertain about the appropriateness of the alternatives, social pressure can be expected to produce considerable conformity.

Notes for Chapter 2

The experimental results reported in this chapter were obtained by John S. Caylor and are reported in full in *Stimulus Ambiguity as a Factor in Conformity,* a dissertation submitted in partial fulfillment of the requirements of the degree of Doctor of Philosophy at the University of Michigan, 1955.

[1] The illustration of the autokinetic effect situation as one in which there is a high degree of stimulus ambiguity is taken from an experiment by Muzafer Sherif and is reported in "An Experimental Approach to the Study of Attitudes," *Sociometry,* I (1937), 90-98. The illustration of the highly structured stimulus situation is taken from the studies of Solomon E. Asch reported in "Studies of Independence and Submission to Group Pressure: I. A Minority of One against a Unanimous Majority," *Psychological Monographs,* Vol. LXX, No. 416.

[2] The classic study of the effect of publicness versus privateness on expression of attitude is reported in Daniel Katz and R. L. Schanck, *Social Psychology* (New York: Wiley, 1938).

[3] S. A. Stouffer, "An Analysis of Conflicting Social Norms," *American Sociological Review,* XIV (1949), 707-717.

[4] C. E. Shannon, "A Mathematical Theory of Communication," *Bell System Technical Journal,* XXVII (1948), 379-423.

[5] The differences in Figure 2 are highly significant from a statistical point of view yielding a chi square with a probability of $<.001$ of having arisen by chance.

[6] All four differences in Figure 5 are highly significant from a statistical point of view. The probability of having arisen by chance is $<.001$ in three cases and is $<.005$ in the fourth.

3

CONFORMITY AND FAMILIARITY

WITH SOURCE AND OBJECT

The expectation was stated in Chapter 1 that the influence of a norm in producing conformity behavior will vary with some aspects of the perceived source of the norm. A norm purported to be from a group with which the subject is closely associated and thus familiar could be expected to produce more conformity than a norm attributed to a more vague and general group. Further, the amount of conformity should vary with the degree of familiarity the subject possesses about the object of the attitude or behavior to be subjected to pressure. This chapter is a report of a study of these two factors in conformity.

An experiment

In the previous chapter conformity was produced by asking a given subject what his attitude might be if no one were to find out what he did, and then asking him what he would do if some reference group were to find out what he had done. The amount of conformity was the amount of change in his attitude under the two sets of circumstances. The two expressions of attitude were taken from the same subject. Conformity can also be inferred from differences in attitude expressed by two different but comparable subjects when one is asked to express an opinion without pressure, and the other is queried under pressure.

In order to investigate the influence of the source of the norm it is only necessary to ask one group of subjects to express an opinion without any attempt to influence that opinion, and ask other comparable groups to express the same opinion after they have been informed of the supposed opinions of a particular norm source. If several different norm sources are employed in this manner, and if the subjects are more intimately associated or more familiar with some than others, then differences in the amount of conformity might be attributable to differences in familiarity with the source or group to which the norm is attributed.

The degree of familiarity with the object of the expressed attitude can be varied in a similar manner. Subjects may be asked to rate a number of objects which have been selected to range from a very familiar to an unfamiliar object. Differences in conformity could thus be attributed to differences in familiarity with the object.

The subjects in this study were members of four sororities on the University of Michigan campus. The girls from each sorority were divided into four groups, a control group and three experimental groups. The three experimental groups were subjected to pressure attributed to three norm sources representing different degrees of familiarity, intimacy of association, or strength of identification. Each of the four groups rated five objects which were chosen to represent different degrees of familiarity. Since each of the four sororities was represented equally in each of the experimental conditions, possible differences between sororities were controlled.

The task for all groups was the same. Each was asked to rate five organizations on a seven-point rating scale ranging from "very good" to "very poor." This vague and somewhat meaningless dimension was chosen deliberately with the expectation that its very indefiniteness would operate to reduce resistance to a norm.

The testing procedures of the four groups differed only as to whether a norm was announced and to whom it was attributed. No norm was announced to the Control Group, so that the attitudes expressed by this group served as a base for measuring the effect of the norm announcement in the other groups. Pressure was exerted by a simple stratagem. For each of the other groups, marks were placed on the rating scales employed, and the marks for one group were purported to show the way in which the five organizations were rated by "most other Michigan students." The group with this source of norm can be referred to as a General Campus Group. In another experimental group the same marks were placed on the rating scale but were attributed to "most other sorority girls," and the group with this source of the norm can be referred to as a General Sorority Group. In the remaining experimental group the same set of marks were attributed to "most other girls in your own group (sorority)." The group with this norm source is referred to as the Own Sorority Group. It was expected that the General Campus Group would represent the least effective norm source, the General Sorority Group would represent more pressure, while the Own Sorority Group would represent the most effective source of the norm.

Of the five organizations in the test, two groups chosen to represent a Close Acquaintance Level were two fraternities with which the girls were closely associated. Two organizations with which the subjects might be expected to be somewhat less familiar were two campus organizations: a student religious association and the local chapter of the National Association for the Advancement of Colored People. These organizations were chosen to represent a Moderate Acquaintance Level. A single group, the Interstate Commerce Commission, was included to represent a Minimum Acquaintance Level. It was expected that the more closely acquainted the girls were with the object of the expressed attitude the less effective would be efforts to produce conformity.

The source of the norm and conformity

The different amounts of conformity produced by the three sources to which the same norm was attributed may be seen in Figure 6.[1] When the norm is attributed to the girls' own sorority, the attitudes expressed are, on the average, nearly one full point more favorable on a seven-point scale. When the norm is attributed to sorority girls in general, the effect is much less dramatic. It produces a shift in attitude of slightly less than half a point. It is somewhat surprising that when the norm is attributed to "most other Michigan students" the effect is nearly as great as when the norm is attributed to "most other sorority girls."

FIGURE 6

CONFORMITY AS A FUNCTION OF THE SOURCE
OF THE NORM

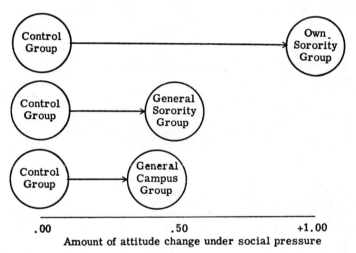

.00   .50   +1.00
Amount of attitude change under social pressure

It is to be noted in interpreting the results of this portion of the experiment that the subjects were members of all three groups to which the norms were attributed. The groups were chosen to represent three degrees of familiarity or closeness of association, and therefore one might be justified in drawing the conclusion that the more familiar the subject is with the source of the norm, the greater the conformity to be expected as a function of social pressure.

This conclusion must be accepted with caution in the light of other dimensions upon which these sources of the norm might be ordered. The differences obtained might be attributed to differences in identification with sources of the norm, and identification might in other circumstances be independent of degree of association. The three groups differ in size. They might differ in prestige for the subjects, and they might differ to the extent that the girls felt the group were competent to judge. Any one of these variables might be alternates to closeness of acquaintance, and it is not possible to distinguish clearly from these results which is the most important.

Familiarity with the object and conformity

It may be seen in Figure 7 that when the object of the expressed attitude is one with which the subjects are closely acquainted (in

FIGURE 7

CONFORMITY AS A FUNCTION OF LEVEL OF
ACQUAINTANCE WITH THE OBJECT

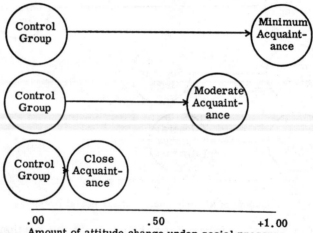

.00   .50   +1.00
Amount of attitude change under social pressure

this case, two fraternities) the announcement of a norm has little effect, producing movement of slightly less than a quarter of a point on a seven-point scale. When the level of acquaintance with the objects is moderate (in this case, a student religious group and the local chapter of the National Association for the Advancement of Colored People), the amount of conformity produced by the announcement of a norm is considerably greater, approximately two-thirds of a point. When the acquaintance level is at a minimum (the Interstate Commerce Commission), maximum conformity is achieved, approximately a full point on a seven-point scale.[2]

Again there is some problem of interpretation. The various object groups were chosen to represent differences in level of acquaintance or familiarity. Acquaintance might be broken down into the amount of previous experience with the object which might have led to the formation of an attitude and the certainty with which the attitude is held. The reader is undoubtedly able to order the object groups in another frame of reference which could account for the differences seen in Figure 7.

Summary

While alternate interpretations are conceivable with respect to both variables manipulated in the study reported in this chapter, two tentative conclusions seem to be justified by the results:

The more familiar the subject is with the reference group to which the norm is attributed, the more effective will be that norm in producing conformity.

The more familiar the subject is with the object of the attitude or behavior to be influenced by a norm, the less effective the pressure toward conformity.

Notes for Chapter 3

This study was carried out almost single-handedly by Harry A. Burdick.

[1] The results presented in Figure 6 are in general highly significant from a statistical standpoint. All three groups were significantly different from the Control Group, the Own Sorority Group was significantly different from the General Sorority Group and from the General Campus Group, but the latter two are not significantly different from each other.

[2] The results presented in Figure 7 are all significant from a statistical standpoint. All differences yield probabilities of arising by chance of $< .01$.

4

CONFORMITY IN RESPONSE

TO GROUP PRESSURE

Greater conformity to group standards is exacted or achieved by closely knit groups. Adolescent cliques manage to impose uniform dress, language and manners in defiance of the standards of the larger social group from which they emerge. The relationships between the attractiveness of a group, its cohesiveness and the pressures toward uniformity have been well documented by Festinger.[1]

This chapter is a report of two experiments in which the attractiveness of the group as the source of the pressure toward conformity was varied. The two studies differed in one respect. In the first, the variable of attractiveness was manipulated without having an influence on conformity. In the second experiment conformity was made instrumental to being liked, and under these circumstances the two groups that differed in attractiveness produced the predicted differences in conformity behavior.

The subject's task

The task the subjects were asked to perform involved a case study which has appeared in journals as the "Johnny Rocco" case.[2] The case is a detailed description of certain factors in the life of a young boy, Johnny, who committed a quite brutal murder of an elderly woman. The subjects in this experiment, after reading about the boy, were asked to make judgments regarding the degree to which Johnny or his environment should be considered responsible for the crime. The subjects were presented a scale made up of seven points where the low end indicated that Johnny should be held completely responsible for his crime and the high end indicated that the environment should be held completely responsible.

The whole case was not presented. The available material was abstracted so that a majority of the subjects would choose positions five or six toward the environmental responsibility end of the scale. Then an effort was made to change their opinion toward personal responsibility on the part of Johnny.

The procedure

The procedure in this experiment is a rather new development in social psychological research that offers a degree of control of social stimulation not previously obtainable in small group research. The innovation is that although the subjects were tested individually, they were completely convinced that they were members of a group. While in actual face-to-face group interaction, each person is subject to a slightly different pattern of stimulation, in this instance each individual was subjected to exactly the same social situation and group pressure.

When a subject appeared, he was escorted to a small room adjoining several other small rooms. His name appeared on the door of his room, and other names appeared on the doors of other rooms. Whether he came alone or with other subjects, he was escorted individually to his own room.

In the small room was a table fitted against the wall. On it were a microphone and a pair of earphones. The earphones were live but the microphone was not—its lead wire was simply taped to the earphone wire but not electrically connected.

The subjects had previously been told that this was to be an experiment in social communication, and each was led to believe that he was one of a group of four subjects. When the subject was seated in his room, he was given a card on which was printed either A − 4 or B − 4, and three items related to the case study. These items were (1) a general statement of the crime committed, (2) a copy of what was purported to be a condensation of the case worker's report on the boy, and (3) a full statement of the meaning of each alternative that could be chosen regarding the degree to which Johnny personally or his environment should be considered responsible for the crime.

The experimenter left the room and then returned after the subjects had had sufficient time to read the case material. Appropriate noises of talking and door opening and closing were made to maintain the impression that four subjects were present. When the experimenter returned, he brought with him the forms on which the subject was to express his opinion about the case and his degree of certainty about his opinion. When the subject had had sufficient time to fill out these forms, they were collected. Then the subject was asked to put on his earphones and get ready to discuss the case.

The earphones were connected to a tape recorder. When the subject was ready, the tape recorder was turned on. The first voice heard was that of the experimenter who explained the procedure. He addressed them as if they were a group and told them that they were to carry out a group discussion over the microphone system. Each person was to speak in turn into the microphone according to his subject number. (All live subjects were assigned the fourth position.) The experiment was explained as one in which a study was being made of the communication process by which groups come to decisions. It was explained that subjects had been separated to avoid contamination which might result from face-to-face communication. The subjects were asked to come to a group decision concerning the problem of responsibility.

At this point in the experiments instructions were designed to create two degrees of attractiveness of groups. Half of the subjects were arbitrarily placed in a group of low attraction and half in a group of high attraction. It will be remembered that each subject had a card with either A − 4 or B − 4 printed on it. The subjects were told that the letter indicated their group and the number indicated their position for speaking. They were told that the members of Group A had been selected from persons whose past record indicated that they would be particularly competent and should be able to do well at this type of task. They were also told that the two groups would be given slightly different tasks to work on in view of the different competence of the two groups. They were also told that some persons from Group A might be moved down to Group B and some persons from Group B might be promoted to Group A. Finally, each subject was asked to keep a tally for the examiners of the positions that each other person took as a check for us on our procedure.

As may be seen the attractiveness of Group A is relative to that of Group B. The difference is based primarily on a statement of differential competence with a possible difference in task attractiveness. It is possible that the instruction concerning the possibility that members of Group B might be promoted to Group A may have contributed to the differential attractiveness of the two groups as well.

At this point the tape recorder was turned off and the experimenter passed from room to room with appropriate tally sheets and rating forms. After all forms were distributed, the experimenter once again turned on the tape recording, and the subjects heard the opinions of what they believed to be three other subjects. The first subject on the recording took position two (near the personal responsibility end). Briefly he gave his reasons for taking this position. The second and third recorded voices took position three and gave their reasons. The live subjects were then given a minute to present their opinions to the group, all speaking at once (if there was more than one present) into the dead microphones. The tape recorder was again turned off and the experimenter collected the tallies. When this was done, the subjects were told to prepare for the next round, and the tape recording was started again. This time all three recorded voices took position three and maintained these positions throughout the remainder of the experiment.

A brief chronological account of the steps in the experiment is as follows:

Step 1—Preliminary instructions and reading of the materials by the subject.

Step 2—Statements of opinion about the case made by the subject and collected by the experimenter. The subject also filled out the form which recorded his degree of certainty about his position at this point. This form was also collected by the experimenter.

Step 3—Further instructions were given, tally sheets were passed out, and the instructions designed to manipulate attractiveness of the groups were delivered.

Step 4—The first attempt to influence the position of the subject was made. The first voice on the recorder took position two and the other two voices took position three. The second statement of the subject's position was collected.

Step 5—The second attempt was made to influence the position of the subject. All three voices took position three. The third position statement on the part of the subject was collected.

Step 6—The third attempt was made to influence the position of the subject with all three voices again taking the third position, and the fourth position statement of the subject was collected.

Step 7—The subject responded to questions designed to determine the effect of the instructions relative to group attractiveness. A fifth and final position statement was collected, and a second statement concerning the certainty with which the subject maintained his position was obtained. It will be noted that these statements of the subject's feelings of certainty about his position are closely related to the measurement of stimulus ambiguity discussed in Chapter 2.

In addition to the above items common to both experiments there were several differences between the two. In the second experiment conformity was made instrumental to being liked by other persons. This was done by adding to the instructions the point that it is common knowledge that persons tend to like one another more, to get along better, when they agree about common problems. This variable was further emphasized by having each subject rate the others on how well the subject liked each of the others and by keeping a tally on how the subject thought the others were rating him. These "liking ratings" were collected as a part of steps four, five and six above.

Results of the First Experiment

In each of the experiments the terminal questionnaire was designed to reveal whether or not the instructions with respect to attractiveness had been effective. There were four questions concerning how well they liked the experiment, how well they liked the other subjects, how much they would like to return for another discussion period, and if they were to return, would they like to return to their own group or another one. With respect to each question Group A was seen as the more attractive group. Subjects in this group liked the experiment and other subjects better and expressed a desire to return in greater numbers than Group B. The subjects in both groups tended to prefer Group A if they were to return.

In the light of these results it is clear that Festinger's principle should be applicable. Briefly restated, the principle is: the more attractive the group, the more cohesive the group, and the more cohesive the group, the more conformity. This principle would lead one to expect the subjects of the High Attraction Group to conform more than the subjects in the Low Attraction Group. The number of subjects showing a high degree of conformity in each group may be seen in Figure 8.

FIGURE 8

CONFORMITY AND ATTRACTIVENESS OF GROUP

High attraction group (A)

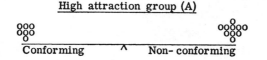

Low attraction group (B)

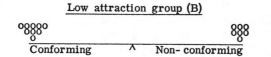

Contrary to expectations from Festinger's principle, there is a slightly greater proportion of conforming subjects in the Low Attraction Group (B). It is clear that under these conditions Festinger's principle does not hold. Furthermore, one of the questions designed originally to ascertain whether the attractiveness instructions were effective, actually permitted an analysis with a curious result. Each subject was asked in the final step of the experiment how well he liked other members of the group. While ten of fifteen subjects in the High Attraction Group (A) expressed a high liking for the others in the group and only six of fourteen subjects in the Low Attraction Group (B) expressed high liking for the other subjects, it is possible to disregard the original classification and form new groupings. Those expressing a high liking for the other subjects can be placed in one group and those expressing a low liking for others in the other group. When this is done and matched against conformity behavior, the results are as shown in Figure 9.[3]

FIGURE 9

CONFORMITY AND LIKING FOR OTHERS IN GROUP

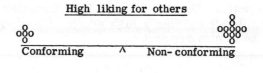

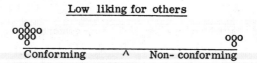

Obviously, non-conforming behavior and high liking for other members of the group are related; and conversely, those who conformed did not like the other members of the group very well at the end of the experiment. This result seems to be exactly the reverse of the expectation from the Festinger principle that the greater the attraction the more cohesive the group, and the more cohesive the group the more conformity one might expect. In all probability, however, another interpretation is more reasonable, and Festinger's principle remains essentially untested. Since the ratings of liking for others were taken at the end of the experimental session, it is quite possible that the conformity came first, and that the subjects who conformed then came to like their supposed fellow subjects less well out of some feeling of having been unduly influenced or pushed around.

It was felt that the characteristic of the situation most needed to make the Festinger principle work was instrumentality. That is, if conformity is seen as being instrumental to being liked, then the relationship between attractiveness and conformity or uniformity would hold. This characteristic could very well have been an implicit aspect of Festinger's instructions and the relationships established between the experimenter and the subjects in the Festinger studies.

Results of the Second Experiment

The differences between the first and second experiment have already been described. In the second one, conformity was made instrumental to being liked by instruction, and the ratings of liking were collected after each attempt to influence the subject as well as at the end of the experiment. This last difference was indeed fortunate, for while the instructions had the effect of producing differences in the attractiveness of the two groups at the outset, subjects changed in their degree of liking for others so rapidly that by the third influence attempt, no difference between the relative attractiveness of the two groups was any longer discernible. Figure 10 shows the relationship between attractiveness and conformity

FIGURE 10

RELATIVE CONFORMITY EARLY IN THE EXPERIMENT
BASED ON ATTRACTIVENESS BY INSTRUCTION

High attraction group (A)

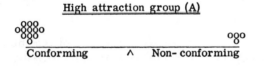

Conforming   ∧   Non- conforming

Low attraction group (B)

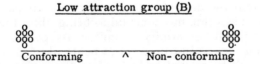

Conforming   ∧   Non- conforming

when attractiveness is categorized on the basis of the original instructions and conformity is measured after the second attempt to influence the opinions of the subjects.

It can be seen that at this point in the experiment, even though there was little residual difference in attractiveness of the two groups, there is a definite trend for the High Attraction Group (A) to conform the most.

If the experimental manipulations are again ignored and the

subjects categorized on the basis of their expressed liking for the others in their group, the relationship is even more pronounced, as may be seen in Figure 11.

FIGURE 11

RELATIVE CONFORMITY AND LIKING FOR OTHERS AT THE END OF THE SECOND INFLUENCE ATTEMPT

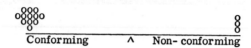

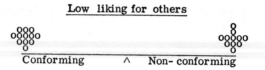

This finding is almost exactly the reverse of that obtained in the first experiment. Here the subject with a high liking for others is much more likely to have conformed than the subject with a low liking for others. The tendency to conform underwent very little further change throughout the remainder of the experiment.

While there are other possible interpretations, these studies seem to indicate that the importance of instrumentality is great. If conformity is seen as being instrumental to being liked, then attractiveness or liking and conformity or uniformity go together. If conformity is not seen as instrumental to being liked, then conformity might very well be related to lowered attractiveness of the group. Even a conformer may resent being influenced and express his resentment by lowering his esteem of those who exerted such an influence.

Certainty of opinion and conformity

It will be recalled that during this experiment an assessment was made of the certainty the subject felt about the position he took after he had read the material provided and before he was subjected to any influence attempt. In Chapter 2 the development of a stimulus ambiguity index was discussed. The conclusion reported was that among individuals, those who see a situation as highly ambiguous are more likely to respond to group pressure and thus conform more, than those who see a situation as relatively unambiguous. Since certainty of opinion is similar if not identical to stimulus ambiguity, the present pair of studies offers another opportunity to examine this relationship.

It can be seen in Figure 12 that the relationship between conformity and certainty of opinion, stimulus ambiguity, is clear. Those

FIGURE 12

CERTAINTY OF OPINION, STIMULUS AMBIGUITY AND CONFORMITY

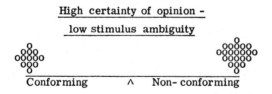

subjects who expressed uncertainty or low certainty about the opinion they expressed after reading the material provided about the Johnny Rocco case showed a strong tendency to conform to the opinions expressed by the other group members. Those subjects who felt relatively certain of the opinion they expressed or the position they took showed a strong tendency toward non-conformity in the face of group pressure. To the extent to which certainty of position and stimulus ambiguity can be equated, this analysis adds a further confirmation of the thesis argued in Chapter 2 that the more ambiguous a stimulus situation the more likely a person is to yield to pressures toward conformity.

Summary

The results of this study seem to lead to these conclusions:

If conformity is seen as being instrumental to being liked, then the expectation that the more attractive a group the more cohesive the group, and the more cohesive the group the more pressure toward uniformity or conformity tends to be fulfilled. If conformity behavior is not seen as instrumental to being liked, then attractiveness and conformity are likely to be inversely related.

In addition, this study seems to support the previously established conclusion that the more ambiguous the stimulus situation appears to the subject, the more likely he will be to conform under social pressure.

Notes for Chapter 4

These variables were examined in a study carried out by Harry A. Burdick and reported in *The Relationship of Attraction, Need-Achievement and Certainty to Conformity under Conditions of a Simulated Group Atmosphere,* a dissertation submitted in partial fulfillment of the requirements for the degree of Doctor of Philosophy at the University of Michigan, 1955.

[1] L. Festinger and J. Thibaut, "Interpersonal Communication in Small Groups," *Journal of Abnormal and Social Psychology,* XLVI (1951), 92-100, and also in L. Festinger, H. Gerard, B. Hymovitch, H. Kelly, and B. Raven, "The influence Process in the Presence of Extreme Deviates," *Human Relations,* V (1952), 327-346.

[2] J. Evans, "Johnny Rocco," *Journal of Abnormal and Social Psychology,* XLIII (1948), 357-383. The same case has been referred to as the Johnny Sandron case in B. Raven, *The Effects of Group Pressures on Opinion, Perception and Communication* (unpublished Ph.D. dissertation, University of Michigan, 1953).

[3] Three subjects failed to give complete data concerning the four questions. Thus the number of subjects in Figure 9 is slightly smaller than the number in Figure 8.

5

THE NORM

AS A SOURCE OF INFORMATION

IN PROBLEM SOLVING

While the child in school is usually enjoined to do his own work and depend only on himself, the individual outside that setting often finds that the group around him is a source of information which can expedite his arrival at the answers to important problems. Cooperative effort is characterized by such behavior. Conformity, previously defined as movement toward a group norm or standard, often occurs in the service of problem solution. It is quite possible that group pressure could be effective with respect to a rating of the "goodness" or "badness" of an organization and still be totally ineffective in a problem-solving situation in which the content of the problem seems much more a matter of fact than a matter of opinion.

41

If a group norm or standard does have an influence on problem-solving behavior, there are many aspects of the situation which might be of interest. As illustrated in Chapter 3, the individual's closeness of association with the group which is the source of the norm might be expected to influence the degree of faith the individual places in the reliability of the norm information. Furthermore, it is possible that in a given situation a norm could be made either more or less effective in producing conformity by statements designed to either enhance or depreciate its value as a source of information. Finally, the extent to which information obtained from a group might be used by an individual in solving a problem could be expected to vary with the level of confidence the individual has in his own solution.

This chapter is a record of attempts to manipulate certain aspects of these three variables in a situation in which a norm attributed to a group could provide information for an individual in a problem-solving situation. All the experiments involved a problem which permitted (a) full control of the amount of information available to the subject, (b) extensive control of the process of problem solving, (c) degrees of correctness of solution, and (d) control of the group contribution to an individual's solution through the announcement of solutions attributed to groups.

The subject's problem

The problem presented to each subject was one of determining the correct order of five arbitrary symbols, such as the following:

$$\$ \qquad \% \qquad \# \qquad \Sigma \qquad \&$$

One of these symbols was "more important" than all others combined. Another was "more important" than the remaining three combined. A third was "more important" than the remaining two combined, and the fourth was "more important" than the fifth. The subject was to order the symbols in terms of importance and was given bits of information in the course of the experiment from which he could learn the correct order. On each of a series of trials in four of the six experiments the subject was presented with three panels of three symbols each, or triads, and he was to rank the panels in importance. When his ranking was completed, he was given an official ranking. Starting with the subject's second trial, his attempted ranking before the official information was given

provided a record of his progress in the solution of the problem.
Table 2 is a sample record from a single trial.

TABLE 2

SAMPLE TRIAL RECORD WITH THREE SYMBOLS

IN TRIAL PANEL

	Triad or panel number		
	(1)	(2)	(3)
	$	&	#
	%	Σ	$
	&	%	Σ
Subject's ranking	1	2	3
Official ranking	2	3	1

From the official information the subject could learn one simple
bit of information and two complex bits. By comparing the sets
ranked second and third he could gain the simple bit of information that $ is more important than Σ since both sets contain % and
&. By comparing the set officially ranked first with the set ranked
second, he could learn that either # or Σ is more important than
both % and &, since $ is common to both sets. By comparing the
set ranked first with the set ranked third, he could find that either
$ or # is more important than both & and % since Σ is common to
both sets. Thus the official information instructed the subject that

$ is greater than Σ
either $ or # is greater than % and &
either # or Σ is greater than % and &

It should be noted that the problem presented to the subjects
can be solved with four bits of information if the four bits are
properly selected. Let us assume that the proper order of arrange-
ment is as follows:

$
Σ
#
%
&

The four bits required to solve the problem are:

$$\$ > \Sigma$$
$$\Sigma > \#$$
$$\# > \%$$
$$\% > \&$$

However, there are six other bits of information which could be provided. They are:

$$\$ > \#$$
$$\$ > \%$$
$$\$ > \&$$
$$\Sigma > \%$$
$$\Sigma > \&$$
$$\% > \&$$

For convenience let us refer to the ten bits of information above as "simple bits." As indicated in Table 2, the official information could provide a large number of complex bits of information. Actually, on a single trial, most subjects were able to work out no more than the simple bits of information, if that much; and over a set of trials, only the simple bits of information were necessary or even very useful in problem solution.

In two of the experiments the information was presented in dyad form rather than in triad form. Table 3 illustrates the information of a single trial in these experiments.

TABLE 3

SAMPLE TRIAL RECORD WITH TWO SYMBOLS

IN TRIAL PANEL

	Dyad or panel number		
	(1)	(2)	(3)
	$\$$	$\&$	$\#$
	$\%$	Σ	$\$$
Subject's ranking	1	2	3
Official ranking	2	3	1

From such a trial the subject could learn one simple bit of information by comparing the dyad ranked first with that ranked second in the official ranking, i.e., that $\% < \#$ because $\$$ was common to both dyads. The complex bit is that either & or $\Sigma < \$$ and %.

This form of information-giving was somewhat simpler and made problem solving easier for the subjects.

The procedure

Each subject had ten initial trials which followed the pattern described—ordering the symbols in the panels and then being told the correct or official ranking for each trial. After the tenth trial the subjects were given a test trial with no official information. This test trial permitted assessment of (a) whether the subject had an ordered scale of any description and (b) the extent to which it was comparable or derivable from the official information.

Next followed the announcement of a group solution or norm which was posted on a blackboard in full view of the subjects. Then a second block of ten trials was administered. In the second series, the ordering designated by the group solution was pointed out on each trial; the subject made his own choices; and finally the official information was provided.

At the end of this block of trials each subject was given a second test, again without any official information. Here the subject could provide a scale which agreed with the announced norm, or he could provide a scale which did not agree with the norm. In the former case he would be classified as a *conformer,* and in the latter case he would be classified as a *non-conformer.* If the subject became confused and presented choices which did not form a scale, he was unclassifiable in either category. The sequence of events just described may be seen in Table 4.[1]

TABLE 4

Training trials		Test		Norm announcement		Training trials with Norm		Test
Training trials	→	Test	→	Norm announcement	→	Training trials with Norm	→	Test

The Experimental Variables and Their Expected Effect on Conformity Behavior

The pattern of work involved in the six studies that follow was reasonably simple. Each of several sets of operations could be manipulated to favor adoption of the norm and produce conformity; or rejection of the norm, in favor of the individual's own solution, and produce non-conformity. By starting with a procedure which favored conformity, and by increasing the number of factors favoring non-conformity from experiment to experiment, it was expected that progressive changes would occur in the number or proportion of experimental subjects demonstrating one or the other kind of behavior.

The Experimental Variables and Their Expected Effect on Conformity Behavior

The source of the norm

The intimacy of association with the group to which the norm is attributed was a variable treated in Chapter 3. It was found that the more intimately associated the individual was with the group, the greater the influence of the norm on the behavior of the individual. In the studies in this chapter it was expected that a norm attributed to the subject's "own group" would have more effect on problem-solving behavior than a norm attributed to "other people." Thus if the norm is attributed to the subject's "own group," this variable should weigh in favor of the use of the group solution, conformity behavior, while attribution of the solution to "other people" should operate to favor the individual's own solution, non-conformity behavior.

Stated value of the norm solution

In order to manipulate the extent to which the stated norm might produce conformity or adoption of the norm, two different statements about the value of the norm were used. When it was desired to apply pressure toward conformity, the statement was:

> Now groups do make mistakes, of course, but it is well known that two heads are better than one, that a group is less likely to make mistakes than is one person.

When it was desired to favor the use of the individual solution over that of the group, the norm was introduced with the statement:

Now you ought to be reminded that the opinions of all people count in something like this no matter how well or how poorly they get along—so it is possible, of course, that this information we are giving you may be a bum steer.

Confidence in one's own solution

There are many possible ways either to strengthen or to shake the individual's confidence in his own tentative solution of a problem. Three different techniques were employed in this respect.

Certainty of own solution. It was established in pretests that if all ten simple bits of information were given in ten trials, even the brightest subject could not solve the problem. A subject given that much information in a very short period of time is certain to be confused and lack confidence in his own solution. This operation, giving ten simple bits of information in ten trials leads to very low confidence in one's own solution and should thus favor adoption of the norm, or conformity behavior.

The subject's confidence in his own partial solution can be increased by giving him only four simple bits of information and by giving him the same four bits more than once so that he has an opportunity not only to learn a part of the solution but to confirm what he thinks he knows. It should be noted that with ten simple bits of information from which to choose, four can be chosen which do not permit complete solution to the problem.

A second way to increase the subject's confidence in his own solution is to increase the number of trials on which information is given. Thus, by increasing the number of trials from ten to twenty-one it becomes possible to give all ten simple bits of information and to have each confirmed at least once. It should be noted that few subjects arrived at a complete and certain solution even under these circumstances. In fact, it is difficult to estimate which of the two operations to increase the subject's confidence in his own solution was the more effective. Both were used where appropriate because the two techniques permit different ways of crediting or discrediting the announced norm solution.

Contradictions between the norm and previous experience. The norm announced at the end of the first practice session could be in complete agreement with the information which had been provided during that period, or it could be made to disagree. Furthermore, it could disagree with respect to only one bit of information which had been provided or it could disagree with as many as ten bits.

With other things equal, a single disagreement between the announced norm and the previous experience of the subject should
produce a small tendency to discredit the norm, to choose to adhere
to one's own solution, and thus to be non-conforming. Ten disagreements should produce a strong tendency to reject the norm
and be a non-conformist.

Contradictions between the norm and subsequent experience.
When the norm was introduced, it was necessary for the subject
to recall what had been learned in the first block of trials in order
to compare it with the norm. If he was somewhat uncertain or hazy
about his own solution, disagreements between that solution and the
one offered by the norm might not be so important. Further discrediting of the norm could be accomplished by producing disagreement between the norm and the official information provided
in the last block of trials. One such disagreement should tend to
discredit the norm rather mildly, while ten such disagreements
should produce a maximum tendency to discredit the norm and
thus a minimum tendency toward conformity.

Reduction in confusion. In four of the experiments the information was presented to the subjects in the form of triads (three
symbols in order) as indicated in Table 2. In two of the experiments
the information was presented in dyads (two symbols in order).
While there is less information in a dyad than in a triad, there is
also less possibility of confusion. Information in dyad form should
therefore serve to produce slightly more confidence in one's own
solution when the norm is presented.

The Experiments

The experiments are presented here in the order of the amount
of conformity expected and obtained.[2]

Experiment 1

In this experiment an effort was made to have a majority of subjects conform to the announced norm. All but one of the manipulations were made to favor conformity behavior. (When the norm
was announced, it was attributed to "other people," thus favoring
non-conformity.) The information was presented in the more
confusing triad form. The norm was given a high value by em-

phasizing in announcing it that a group is less likely to make mistakes than is an individual. Furthermore the subject was presented with ten bits of information in ten trials, an operation which produced more confusion than information. Finally, there was no disagreement between the announced norm and the information provided in either block of trials. Thus, all variables but the group to which the norm was attributed were employed in the direction of producing conformity behavior. The results may be seen in Figure 13—where the subjects in the center produced scales which could not be classified.

FIGURE 13

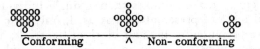

Conforming   ∧   Non-conforming

Experiment 2

In this experiment a single change was made to alleviate the pressure toward conformity. Instead of ten bits of information in the first ten trials, the number was reduced to four and each was confirmed at least once. Otherwise the experiment did not differ from Experiment 1. Thus the norm was attributed to "other people," but the statement was made that the group was less likely to make mistakes than a single individual. The information was presented in the confusing triad form, and the information given in both blocks of trials was not in disagreement with the norm. Therefore, two factors operated to produce non-conformity, and all the others operated to produce conformity. The results are shown in Figure 14, where there was a small but definite shift in the

FIGURE 14

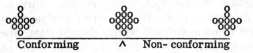

Conforming   ∧   Non-conforming

direction of non-conformity as compared to the results in Experiment 1. In fact, the number of conformers and non-conformers is exactly equal.

Experiment 3

This study was identical to Experiment 2, except that the norm solution disagreed with the official information concerning one bit of information in the first block of trials and one bit in the second block. Since only four bits were presented in the first block and these four were verified or confirmed at least once each, this single disagreement was expected to produce considerable skepticism about the value of the norm and was expected to produce more non-conformity than had been obtained in the first two experiments. To recapitulate the conditions in Experiment 3, the norm was attributed to "other people," but the statement was made that a group was less likely to make mistakes than a single individual; the confusing triad form of presentation was used; only four bits of information were presented in the first block of ten trials; and there was one disagreement between the announced norm and the information given in the first block of trials and another disagreement between the announced norm and the information given in the second block of trials. The results in Figure 15 show more non-conformers than conformers, eleven as compared to nine, for the

FIGURE 15

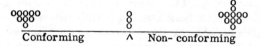

first time shifting the balance in favor of the individual solution as against adoption of the norm solution.

Experiment 4

A number of differences exist between Experiment 4 and Experiment 3, but the changes were designed only to increase the number of non-conformers. In this study the norm was attributed to the subject's "own group," which should have operated to produce a greater tendency to adopt the norm solution than its attribution to "other people." However, this effect should have been effectively cancelled by the omission in Experiment 4 of the norm-enhancing statement, i.e., that the group is less likely to make a mistake than the individual. Again, only four bits of confirmed information were presented in the initial training period, but this time confidence in the individual solution was bolstered by presenting the information in the less confusing dyad form. Furthermore, while there was no disagreement between the norm and the information presented in the first block of trials, the second block was increased in number from ten to twenty, and six bits of information presented during this block disagreed with the announced norm. The net effect should have been to discredit the norm and increase the subject's confidence in his own solution, thus creating more non-conformity. As can be seen in Figure 16, the results were as expected. Only one-third of the subjects adopted the norm solu-

FIGURE 16

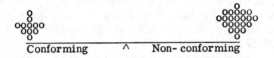

tion and conformed, while the remaining two-thirds chose to stay with their own solution. It will be noted that when the information was presented in dyad form, all subjects were classifiable as either conformers or non-conformers.

Experiment 5

The procedure in this study was designed to produce more dependence on the individual solution or non-conformity than in Experiment 4. To accomplish this, the subject's self confidence in his own solution was increased by increasing the number of trials in the first training period from ten to twenty-one and by presenting ten bits of information, all of which were confirmed, instead of four. The norm, when announced, was made to disagree with

FIGURE 17

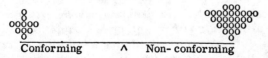

six bits which had been presented in the first training period. Otherwise the operations were the same as in the previous experiment; the norm was attributed to the subject's "own group," no statement was made about the value of the norm, and the information was presented in the less confusing dyad form. As may be seen in Figure 17, the proportion of non-conforming subjects was increased slightly in comparison with Experiment 4.

Experiment 6

Experiment 6 was an effort to see if the norm solution could be completely discredited. Apart from presenting the information in the triad form, all operations were manipulated to favor nonconformity. The norm was attributed to "other people," and was further discredited by indicating when it was presented that it might prove to be a "bum steer." The subject's confidence in his own solution was augmented by presenting only four bits of confirmed information in the initial block of ten trials, and the norm was made to disagree with the official information on all ten initial trials as well as all ten trials following the presentation of the norm. It is difficult to see how any subject could adopt the norm solution under these circumstances, but as can be seen in Figure 18, four subjects continued to conform, while five were confused.

FIGURE 18

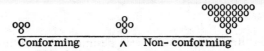

Conforming   ∧   Non- conforming

Summary

The six studies show that in this setting little difficulty was experienced in manipulating the number of conformers and nonconformers, as may be seen in Figure 19, which summarizes the results of this chapter. The studies were not designed to permit clear relative values to be assigned to the manipulated variables. The results, however, do point clearly to several generalizations.

The effectiveness of a given norm may be either enhanced or reduced by attributing either high or low value to it.

A subject's use of a norm to derive a solution in an area with which he is not completely familiar will vary inversely with the degree of confidence he has in his own solution to the problem.

The greater the disagreement between the norm and the subject's own experience, the less effective will be the norm in modifying the subject's behavior.

FIGURE 19

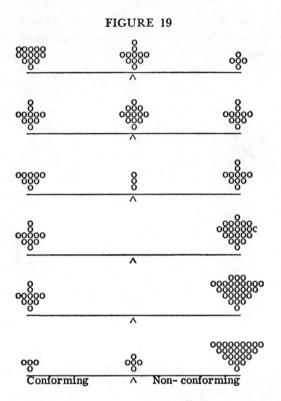

Conforming   ∧   Non- conforming

The greater the disagreement between the norm and another source designated as "official" or correct, the less effective will be the norm in modifying the subject's behavior.

Notes for Chapter 5

Experiments 1, 2, 3, and 6 were joint efforts in which the primary responsibility was carried by Robert Birney, John Caylor, Patricia O'Connor and Harry Burdick. Experiment 4 was largely the work of Patricia O'Connor, and Experiment 5 was largely the work of Harry Burdick.

[1] There were occasional minor variations in this general procedure. These variations are indicated with respect to particular experiments later in the chapter.

[2] These experiments were actually run in the order 1, 2, 6, 3, 4, and 5.

6

CONFORMITY

AND CONFLICT OF NEEDS

Conformity is most certain to occur when there is a strong need and the situation requires conformity behavior in order to satisfy that need. In many situations conformity behavior leads to the satisfaction of one need, while non-conformity behavior leads to the satisfaction of quite a different need. In many situations the behavior which occurs will be *selected* in terms of the relative strengths of the needs involved. Furthermore, the strength of a need in a person at a given moment may well depend in part on the character of the situation. Many human needs are stronger in one situation than in another. Therefore, conformity and non-conformity behavior may fluctuate from time to time, depending on the strengths of the needs that serve the two classes of behavior and in situations which superficially appear to have much in common.

An example of a conflict of needs might be the problem faced rather frequently by most college students. As a student is leaving the dining hall on a Thursday evening, a group of students ask him to go with them to a local movie. This student is immediately in conflict, for, as is true of most college students, he has a strong desire to make good grades. There is a psychology examination on Friday for which he has studied extensively. He had planned to spend the evening in additional preparation in order to be sure that he had the material under complete command. This particular group of students, who have invited him to accompany them, is a group to which he feels strongly attached and whose friendship he values highly. A diagram of the conflict situation in which he finds himself is shown in Figure 20. The two instrumental acts, studying for the examination and joining the group at the movie, are mutually incompatible. The satisfaction of one need precludes the satisfaction of the other.

Which path will he take? What choice will he make? Other things being equal he will choose the alternative which satisfies the stronger need. If his needs for Achievement are high and his needs for Affiliation are low, he will most certainly beg off the invitation and maintain his resolve to study for the psychology examination. If his needs for Achievement are somewhat less strong and his needs for Affiliation are very high, he will certainly skip the books in favor of his friends.

If the two needs are approximately in balance, our student will be undecided. If this is the case, any casual event which acts to arouse and thus to heighten one or the other of the two needs will probably be the determining factor in his choice. Suppose that as he is attempting to make up his mind, another student is seen in the distance and someone remarks, "Let's move off before that creep tries to tag along." Such a situation would be likely to arouse our student's needs for Affiliation enough to determine his choice. On the other hand, if the conversation happens to turn to grades and jobs, it is probable that the consequent heightening of his needs for Achievement will result in a strengthened resolve to resist temptation, forego the movie and the company of his friends, and return to his books.

FIGURE 20
CONFLICT OF NEEDS

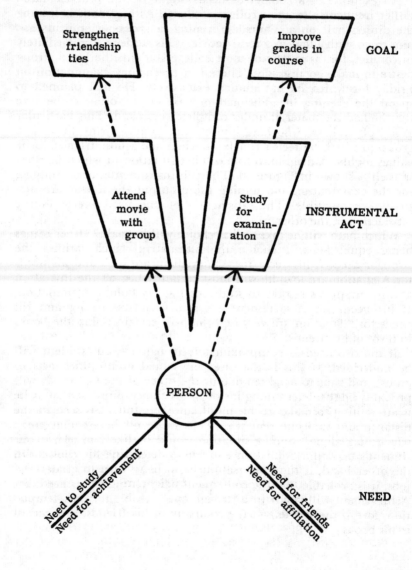

A Laboratory Experiment on Needs in Conflict

The necessary elements of a laboratory experiment to demonstrate choice between conformity and non-conformity behavior in a conflict situation analogous to the one described above can be stated as follows:

1. It is necessary to be able to measure at least two human motives with sufficient reliability to permit prediction on the basis of their relative strengths.

2. A situation must be constructed which will arouse both motives.

3. Goal states must be provided which are appropriate to each of the motives.

4. Conformity behavior must be clearly instrumental to the achievement of one goal state, non-conformity must be clearly instrumental to the other.

5. The two instrumental acts, the one leading to achievement of one goal through conformity and the other leading to the achievement of the other goal through non-conformity, must be mutually incompatible.

Measures of need for Achievement and need for Affiliation

The measures of human needs employed in this experiment bear some description. The technique of measurement is that developed by David C. McClelland and his associates over a number of years.[1] The basic procedure is essentially as follows: Some interesting human need is selected. Let us choose for example the need for Achievement. A group of people are enlisted to serve as subjects in an experiment. They are divided into at least two sub-groups which are to be handled differently. One group is given "achievement oriented" instructions. It is explained that they are to be given a test. Various instructions are used, aimed at creating the impression that the test is to measure ability, that the score is an important index of success, and that people who score high on this test do well at important tasks. It is made clear that the subjects' performances on the test will have an important bearing on something that may happen to them. The second sub-group is handled in the same way in every respect except for the explanation of the purpose of the test. This group is given "task oriented" instructions. The person in charge explains that he is interested in the test itself, that they are to try to do well, but no one is interested in how well the individual subject does on the test.

The test consists of a series of pictures. In general, the pictures portray people who may be doing something, but the pictures are selected on the basis of relative ambiguity and variety of possible interpretations.

The subjects are asked to tell a brief story about each picture and are guided by a few simple questions, such as, "What is happening?" and "What are the people thinking?" It is then possible to score these stories for "achievement imagery" and other characteristics indicating that people in the pictures and in the stories are striving to achieve excellence or to do well with respect to abstract, self-set standards.

It is found that stories written by the subjects in the group given "achievement oriented" instructions contain more achievement imagery than stories written by subjects in the "task oriented" group. From this fact the following inference is made: if two people write stories in a standard situation, if the two sets of stories are scored for achievement imagery, if one person receives a very high need for Achievement score and the other receives a very low score, then the two people represent one with a high need for Achievement and one with a low need for Achievement. It is thought that the need for Achievement score measures the frequency and intensity of striving to meet self-imposed standards of excellence in achievement. It is believed that this human motive is developed as a function of early independence training. In the situation of the college student in conflict over whether to study for the examination or to join his friends for an evening at the movies, need for Achievement would be a measure of the strength of his need to study for the examination in order to achieve a high grade.

A measure of need for Affiliation has been developed in a similar manner. A group of subjects are induced to write stories in response to a set of relatively ambiguous pictures after an effort has been made to arouse a need to be with and to be liked by other people. A second group writes similar stories in response to the same pictures after instructions which are "task oriented." Both groups of stories are then scored for "affiliation imagery" or elements in the stories having to do with needs for close interpersonal relations. Two subjects achieving widely different scores on this dimension when they have written stories under identical conditions are assumed to differ markedly in the strength or intensity of their needs for Affiliation. Thus a need for Affiliation score presumably measures the strength of our student's need to join his friends for the evening.

It should be noted that this technique of developing measures for human motives permits the identification of people who have a strong need for Achievement or a strong need for Affiliation. Something very positive may be said about each. However, little information is obtained concerning persons who do not show appropriate imagery in these situations. If an individual exhibits little achievement imagery when the situation demands it, it would seem that such a person is not characterized by a high need for Achievement. But no positive information is obtained about what the motives of such a person are in the situation. Consequently when need for Achievement and need for Affiliation are measured in this way, predictions can be made with a degree of assurance only about people who make high scores. Little can be said about those who do not make high scores and are designated as being low in need for Achievement or low in need for Affiliation.

The experiment

Needs for Achievement and needs for Affiliation were measured on a large group of undergraduate students at the University of Michigan. Given reliable measures of two human motives, the following procedure was devised to fulfil the other four requirements for a laboratory experiment analogous to the conflict situation described earlier:

Students were asked to volunteer to serve as subjects in this experiment. They were asked to choose a friend and to come to the experiment in pairs. A total of fifty-six pairs or a total of one hundred twelve women participated, and twenty-six pairs or a total of fifty-two men volunteered.

As soon as the subjects arrived, the pairs were separated and each member of the pair was taken to a different room. The task was presented as one in which one member of each pair was asked to *encode* a list of words. This was a simple process of scrambling the order of the letters in a prescribed way. It was explained that the partner would have the task of *decoding* the words by rearranging the letters in the proper order. Both groups, and thus both members of each pair, performed exactly the same task under exactly the same instructions. Subjects were unaware of this duplicity until all data had been collected. At that time the whole experiment was explained.

Approximately ten subjects were present in a room at any one experimental session. The task was to encode as many words as possible in a three minute period. In order to arouse a high need for Achievement, the task was presented as a contest to see who within the group could encode the largest number of words in the time allowed. They were told that there would be six such periods or contests.

It was further explained that after the first work period the list of words that had been encoded would be taken across the hall where the partner was waiting. During the second work period the partner would have the task of unscrambling this list of words or decoding as many of them as possible. It was explained (falsely) that the friend was in competition also, and that the partner's score would be the percentage of the list he received that he succeeded in unscrambling. Thus the partner's task was made the more difficult the larger the number of words encoded by the subject. The friend's competitive situation was mentioned in the original instructions but was not stressed at that time.

At the end of the second three-minute period, what was represented as the partner's first effort was returned to the subject. He was asked to check the list to be sure that the partner had recovered the correct word and then to calculate the percentage correct. The list which was returned to the subject at this point was, of course, not genuine. A number of such lists had been prepared in advance with varying numbers of supposedly decoded words on them. The experimenters merely collected the first products of the first work period of the subjects, chose a list of decoded words from the prepared supply that was either half or slightly less than half as long as the list encoded by each subject. This fake list was returned to the subject for checking and scoring and was represented as being the product of the partner's efforts.

The first two work periods, then, were carried out under conditions aimed at producing high need for Achievement, without any attempt to arouse need for Affiliation other than those contained in the original instructions. At the end of the second work period, however, each subject received for the first time what was purported to be his partner's list with approximately fifty per cent of the words decoded. There was no way for the subject to know whether this represented either a good or a bad performance on the part of the partner.

At the end of the third work period each subject again received a list of words with approximately half of the words decoded.

At the end of the fourth work period the list returned to the subject was like the previous ones, but it bore a request, presumably from the friend, to *please slow down*. This request was intended to maximize the conflict between need for Achievement which could be satisfied by trying hard to win in the subject's own group, and need for Affiliation. To satisfy that need, it was necessary for the subject to reduce his output, and allow the partner to score a high percentage by having fewer words to decode. A subject could try to win in his own group or he could deliberately slow down and lose in order to give his friend a chance to win.

At the end of the fifth trial the subjects were told that the sixth trial would be the last, and that their friend would not be required to decode the words encoded on this last trial. Thus the subject was again free to work as hard as possible to win in his own group without jeopardizing his friend's chances.

In brief, this experiment permitted four encoding trials without appreciable pressure from the phantom partner during which it was hoped that the output would become relatively stable. Then followed a trial on which the pressure to slow down for the sake of a friend was maximum. Finally came a trial during which this pressure was removed. A small group of subjects, approximately every fifth one, worked throughout the series without any appeal from the friend. This group was intended to provide a standard performance against which to measure the effect of the appeal.

Two other procedures were used. One was intended to heighten the need for Affiliation for all subjects. The other was employed to determine the effectiveness of some aspects of the procedures used.

Affiliation arousal. While the very structure of the situation described above should have been adequate to arouse the affiliative motive, one additional step was taken. Before beginning the task each subject was given a list of personal traits. He was asked to indicate the extent to which each trait applied to himself, to his friend, and how he thought the friend would be rating him. This procedure closely approximates that used in the original development of the scoring system for the need for Affiliation. The adjectives on which the ratings were made were: sympathetic, dominant, cheerful, friendly, compliant, hostile, warm, suspicious, approval-seeking, and trusting.

Post-experimental questionnaire. This questionnaire was designed to ascertain how well the experimental operations worked. It revealed that very few subjects suspected the nature of the experiment. Very few subjects were suspicious of the source of the materials purported to come from the partner. Those subjects whose answers indicated any suspicion at all were treated separately, and no differences could be found in their performances which could be attributed to this suspicion.

The Results

The effects of social pressure on performance

The first question to be asked is, "Did this tricky manipulation of social pressure have any effect on the performance of the subjects?" A picture of the performances of three classes of subjects may be seen in Figure 21. The three curves portray the performances of all men, the small number of women who were subjected to no appeal from the phantom partner, and the larger number of women who were subjected to social pressure on the fifth trial.

First, the experiment can be called successful because the expected dip in output as a response to the plea from the friend is apparent in the curve for the women subjected to pressure. Enough of these women subjects were willing to sacrifice their own chance of winning in order to help their partner to produce a noticeable effect. The curve rises again on the sixth trial when the pressure is removed.[2] This result makes possible an analysis of who did and who did not yield to social pressure among the members of this group.

Before such an analysis is made, however, there are two other aspects of these results worthy of brief discussion. The small group of women who were not subjected to social pressure also reduced their output slightly and then increased it again on the sixth trial. The curve appears to mirror the effect on the women who were subjected to social pressure, but the size of the effect is smaller. This small dip in performance during the fifth work period appears to be the result of changes in the group atmosphere. During the first four work periods the competition was intense and all subjects were working very hard at the task. On the fifth trial the general atmosphere of tension in the room tended to slacken as many of the subjects slowed down in response to the supposed appeal from their partners. This tension picked up again somewhat on the sixth trial. While there was no verbal communication to which this general atmosphere effect could be attributed, the general feeling of tension did vary, and it appears to have had a small

FIGURE 21

PERFORMANCE AS A FUNCTION OF
SOCIAL PRESSURE TO CONFORM

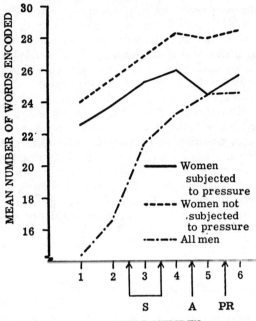

S = Points at which Partner's Score was Presented
A = Point at which Appeal to "Slow Down" was made
PR = Point at which Social Pressure was Removed

effect even on those women who were not subject to any formal appeal from the partner.

A second result of interest is the apparent fact that the women subjects respond to the social pressure of a plea to *please slow down,* but the men do not. This finding fits into a general pattern of sex differences in need for Achievement and need for Affiliation. Our culture places a high value on independence in men, and they tend to receive early and consistent independence training. If they do not, they are regarded as a "mother's boy" or a "sissy," and neither label is considered desirable. The result is that our culture tends to build into men high needs for Achievement, high striving to meet standards of excellence, especially in competitive situations. In a conflict situation with two paths leading to the satisfaction of different needs, Achievement or Affiliation, the men appear to have chosen Achievement almost without exception.

Our culture does not tend to place such universal requirements for early and enduring independence on women. The passive, dependent girl is not subjected to negative social sanctions as a rule. In fact, girls are rather consistently rewarded for such behavior. While no such generalization is applicable to all girls and women, the effects of this cultural difference in the treatment of girls and boys may well be the explanation of the apparent fact that the men did not respond at all to social pressure, while enough of the women did respond to produce a discernible effect.

The failure of the men as a group to respond to pressure makes it useless to attempt to predict which men would respond and which would not from measures of need for Achievement and need for Affiliation. The same is true of the group of women who were not subjected to social pressure. The slight tendency to respond to the variation in the atmosphere of tension would not be predictable from measures of the two motives. Therefore, further analyses were confined to the records of the eighty-nine women who were subjected to social pressure.

Motive pattern and conformity

Since eighty-nine women as a group did yield to social pressure to a significant degree, it is possible to proceed with an analysis of the tendency to yield to the pattern of motives as measured by the techniques described earlier.

The argument is that a person who is high in need for Achievement and low in need for Affiliation will continue to encode words as fast as possible, continue to try to win in her own group, and ignore the plea to slow down. On the other hand, the person who is high in need for Affiliation and low in need for Achievement will be willing to forego any chance of competing successfully in her own group, and will choose to reduce her own output so that the partner will have a chance to win by decoding a smaller number but higher percentage of the words given her.

The diagram used earlier in reference to the student in conflict over whether to join his friends for the evening or to return to books can now be revised to fit this experimental situation. It may be seen in Figure 22. The situation allows little in the way of

FIGURE 22

THE EXPERIMENTAL CONFLICT SITUATION

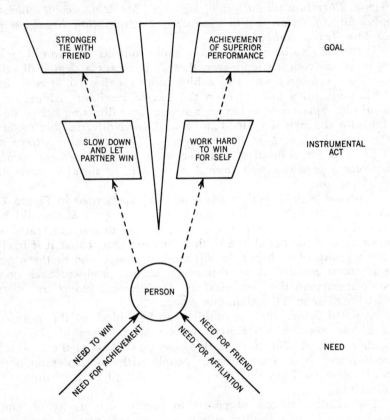

compromise. Both needs cannot be satisfied at the same time and with the same performance. The subject must make a choice—work furiously and try to achieve the satisfaction of winning, or slow down and try to achieve the gratification associated with helping a friend achieve a desired goal.

Who can be expected to work furiously is clear. Any of the subjects in this experiment making a high score on the test of need for Achievement and also making a low score on the test for need for Affiliation should work hard to win in her own group. In Figure 22 this person would be represented as one with a strong force directing her toward the goal of winning in her own group and a weak force directing her to slow down for the sake of her friend. *Therefore the pattern of high need for Achievement and low need for Affiliation would indicate a predisposition toward non-conformity to social pressure.*[3]

It should also be easy to choose those subjects who would yield to pressure from a friend even though it meant a degree of self-sacrifice. A subject who had a high score on the test of need for Affiliation and a low score on the test of need for Achievement would be represented as having a strong force directing her to slow down for the sake of a friend and a weak force directing her toward the goal of winning in her own group. *Therefore the pattern of high need for Affiliation and low need for Achievement would indicate a predisposition toward conformity to social pressure in this situation.*

A person high in both needs would be represented in Figure 22 as having strong forces directing her to each goal. She would be in real conflict of a very intense sort. No prediction can really be made concerning her choice in this situation except that it is likely that a group of such people will tend to choose one or the other goal about equally. If so, this group should produce fewer non-conformers than the high need for Achievement group and more than the high need for Affiliation group.

As noted before, little or nothing can be said about the meaning of a low score, which merely denotes the absence of the need being measured. Therefore, nothing can be said about the expected performance in this situation of people with low scores on both need measures. They shall therefore be omitted from further consideration.

The relative success of efforts to predict conformity or non-conformity in this conflict situation from measures of need for Achievement and need for Affiliation may be seen in Figure 23. Of those subjects who had a high need for Achievement score and a low need for Affiliation score and thus had a relatively stronger force directing them to try to win in their own group, approximately three-fourths chose to continue to work as hard and as fast as possible. Of those who had a high need for Affiliation score and

FIGURE 23

PATTERNS OF CONFORMITY AS DETERMINED BY NEEDS

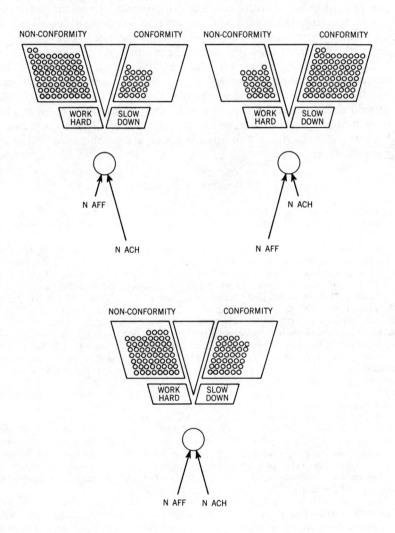

a low need for Achievement score, and thus were strongly motivated to conform, approximately three-fourths did in fact slow down in an effort to aid the friend. Those subjects who were in real conflict, those who were high in both needs, demonstrated their conflict by choosing between the two courses of action nearly equally. Sixty per cent of these subjects chose non-conformity to social pressure.[4]

In summary, then, and with respect to women subjects only as far as this experimental demonstration is concerned, the conclusion can be drawn that *in a situation where conformity is instrumental to the satisfaction of one need and non-conformity to another, the resultant behavior will depend on the relative strengths of the two needs or motives.* And if this conclusion may be generalized, it may be said that conformity behavior will often occur when the situation is such that the satisfaction of any strong need of the person requires conformity behavior as an instrumental act to the satisfaction of the goal of that need.

Notes for Chapter 6

This study of conformity and non-conformity as a function of relative strength of needs in conflict was truly a joint project in conception, formulation and execution. Those chiefly responsible were Robert Birney, Harry Burdick, John Caylor, Patricia O'Connor and Joseph Veroff. The latter was irreplaceable in the handling of the need measures.

[1] See D. C. McClelland, J. W. Atkinson, R. A. Clark, and E. L. Lowell, *The Achievement Motive* (New York: Appleton-Century-Crofts, 1953) and J. W. Atkinson, *Motives in Fantasy, Action, and Society* (New York: D. Van Nostrand Company, Inc., 1958).

[2] If conformity is defined as occurring when a subject's score decreases between trials four and five and increases between trials five and six, then a greater proportion of conformers occurred in the group subjected to social pressure than in the group not subjected to social pressure. This result is significant statistically ($p = <.01$) in spite of the slight dip and rise in the performance of the group not subjected to social pressure.

[3] The designations of *high* and *low* with respect to either need is achieved by the simple expedient of dividing the distribution of scores approximately in the middle. Any subject whose score on the need for Achievement test is above this point is designated as being *high* in need for Achievement. Any subject whose score is below this point is designated as being *low*. Thus the designations of high and low are relative rather than absolute. Since there were eighty-nine subjects in the group with which we are concerned, there are approximately twenty-two subjects in each of the groups formed by classifying each person as being high or low on each need measure.

[4] A two-by-two-by-two table which categorizes subjects as either high or low on each need and as being either a conformer or a non-conformer on the basis of performance in the situation, yields a Chi Square of 13.29 which would have occurred by chance with a probability of $<.01$.

7

CONFORMITY

AS A FLEXIBLE HABIT

Habits, like the needs for achievement and affiliation, are a class of predispositions to behave in a particular way in a certain situation. Habits are acquired through experience in the same or similar situations. Between several possible ways of behaving in a given situation, a person will tend to choose, through learning, that particular way of behaving which most often works or leads to reward. Because habits are basically flexible, they are subject to change through instruction, further training, or through a change in the pattern of reward. In this chapter the concern is with the flexible habit of conforming or not conforming in particular situations.

Since the emphasis is on the flexible character of habits, perhaps a word should be said about some classes of behavior which appear to be inflexible. Some habits, like smoking, appear to be persistent not because the habit itself is inflexible, but because the goal or reward persists. Anyone could probably "break the habit" quickly and easily if means were found to remove all of the pleasure. Thus, if the goal were removed, the habit would probably show little tendency to persist.

A predisposition, which looks like a habit but which is not, has been called "fixated" behavior by Norman R. F. Maier.[1] Under conditions of frustration an organism may seize upon the most available act, the easiest thing to do under the circumstances, and persist in performing that act each time the situation is met. Fixated behavior is marked by its persistence even after the source of frustration is removed, or even when the behavior leads inevitably to punishment. Fixated behavior is inflexible and is not to be defined as a "habit."

It is believed that some ways of behaving become so general in a given person that they may be described as character traits. There is no good evidence that such traits are in fact inflexible. They may persist because they are effective, as smoking persists because of the satisfaction derived from it. They may in rare instances persist because they were developed in the presence of severe frustration. It is likely, however, that most such traits may be modified as are ordinary habits when the conditions persistently warrant change, when an alternate way of behavior would be demonstrably more effective.

Some habits are so well practiced that they become automatic. Driving habits are a good example. They may be somewhat more difficult to change because of the apparent absence of conscious control, but they still remain sufficiently flexible in most people that automobile manufacturers are able to change the form and location of gadgets as well as the pattern of operation needed to manipulate the vehicle.

Human behavior is enormously plastic and modifiable. The most direct approach is through verbal instruction. One can simply issue a set of orders as does a military commander, or write a set of instructions as does the maker of do-it-yourself kits. The behavior desired is very likely to occur. It is also true that a more indirect approach can be effective. People can and do acquire habits or predispositions without being aware that their behavior is being changed or without being aware of the nature of the habits they have acquired.

Tendencies toward conformity or non-conformity might thus be developed as a function of consistent reward for one or the other class of behavior. Furthermore, this could happen without the person being aware that his tendency to conform or not to conform is being influenced in any way. In this chapter, two kinds of experiments are described which were designed to produce conformity and non-conformity behavior without the subject's awareness.

For a person to be unaware of the nature of the influence which is being exerted on his behavior, it is necessary to divert his attention to some other aspect of the situation. This requirement is equivalent in some sense to the classic skill of the prestidigitator who systematically diverts the attention of the audience from the point at which the trick is actually being accomplished. The following two types of experiment represent efforts to involve groups of people in games or tasks which appear on the surface to be unrelated to conformity or non-conformity behavior. Each involves the creation of an elaborate false cover to divert the individual from the real purpose of the experiment.

An Extra-Sensory Perception Experiment as a Cover for the Learning of Conformity and Non-Conformity Behavior

In this study, eighty-two students were invited to participate in a test of extra-sensory perception. The experiment was actually carried out twice with one minor difference in procedure between the two versions. The students came to the laboratory in groups of ten in the first version of the experiment and in groups of seven in the second version.

Each group was confronted with a general explanation of the nature of extra-sensory perception. The experiment was explained as a test of whether they could guess what someone in another room was thinking. The actual procedure was the following:

The groups were taken to the floor above and some distance away in the building and were shown the "sending room." This room was occupied by a man who was designated as a "sender." In one version of this study the "sender" had before him a small panel with five buttons labeled A, B, C, D, and E. In the second version there were eight buttons labeled A, B, C, D, E, F, G, and H.

In the "sender's" room was also a buzzer. Wires attached to the buttons and to the buzzer were conspicuous and ran through a hole in the wall.

The procedure of the experiment, as well as its ostensible purpose, was explained at this point. Subjects were told that when they returned to the experimental room, they would see a panel of five lights or eight lights depending on which version of the experiment they were in. The lights would be labeled to correspond with the buttons in the "sender's" room. Furthermore, there would be in the experimental room a button to sound the buzzer in the "sender's" room as a signal to the "sender."

There were to be a series of trials. On each trial the experimenter with them in the experimental room was to press the button as a signal for the "sender" to start thinking about what button or buttons he was about to press. Each subject was to try to "receive" the message and guess its content. When the guesses had all been recorded, the experimenter was to sound the buzzer again as a signal for the "sender" to actually press buttons, light the lights, and reveal which ones he had been thinking about.

The group was then taken back to the original experimental room. They were given the additional instruction that on each trial they were to give their guesses in order and aloud so that the experimenter could record them. It was explained that in order to make things "fair," each person in the group would give his guess first once, and on the following trial the next person would give his guess first, and so on. In other words, with the ten (or seven) subjects seated in a semi-circle, they could be numbered 1 through 10 or 1 through 7. On the first trial the order of "guessing" would be 1, 2, 3, 4, 5, 6, 7, 8, 9, and 10. On the second trial it would be 2, 3, 4, 5, 6, 7, 8, 9, 10, and 1. On the third trial it would be 3, 4, 5, 6, 7, 8, 9, 10, 1, 2, and so forth. The order of "guessing" in the groups of seven was rotated in the same manner. This procedure was continued through twenty trials in one case and twenty-one trials in the other. Thus each person reported his "guess" twice in each position in the first version of the experiment and three times in each position in the second version.

The "sender" in the "sender's room" was of course a false front. He did not participate in the experiment beyond the visit to his room, and his panel of buttons and buzzer were not really connected to anything. Instead, another man was stationed in a room adjacent to the experimental room. An opening between the two rooms, fitted with a small door which was fastened, permitted the observer to hear everything that went on. He had in his room a panel of buttons, connected to the panel of lights in the experimental room. Instead of a buzzer, which could have been heard by the experimental subjects, he had a small light serving as a signal when the experimenter pressed his signal button. On each trial he was able to tabulate the "guesses" made by the group of subjects and decide which light or lights to turn on, depending upon which kind of behavior, conformity or non-conformity, he wished to "reward."

The first subject to report his "guess" had no choice except to choose a light which had not been chosen by another subject. The second subject did have a choice, however. He could choose a light which had not yet been mentioned or he could choose a light already chosen by someone else.

A maximum of conformity would be represented by the group of subjects slavishly following the leader, with every person choosing whatever light was chosen by the first person. A maximum of non-conformity would be represented by an instance in which every subject went his own way and chose a different light. This condition is theoretically possible in the second version of the experiment, in which there were eight lights and seven subjects, but not in the first version in which there were only five lights and ten people in the group. Nevertheless, most subjects, on most trials, in both experiments, had an opportunity to choose between lights more or less frequently chosen by subjects who preceded him in order of reporting "guesses."

It was the task of the man hidden in the adjacent room to tabulate the guesses and reward conformity behavior if the group had been chosen as a Conformity Group or to reward non-conformity behavior if the group of subjects had been arbitrarily designated as a Non-Conformity Group. This could be done simply by turning on a light or lights which had been chosen by few, if any, subjects in a Non-Conformity Group, or by flashing lights chosen by many subjects in a Conformity Group. Thus he was able to "reward" individual decision in one set of groups and a "follow the leader" choice in the other set of groups.[2]

It should be noted that the subjects were wholly unaware of the true nature of the experiment. Furthermore, the differences in pattern of choice of lights to be lighted in a Conformity Group as opposed to a Non-Conformity Group was barely detectable to someone with knowledge of the procedure observing the experiment in the experimental room. The question then is, can such a subtle, barely detectable and covert difference in the way two groups are treated produce a noticeable difference in the tendency to choose a light chosen by other members of the group or to choose one that has not been or has seldom been chosen by other members of the group?

FIGURE 24

LEARNING OF CONFORMITY AND NON-CONFORMITY

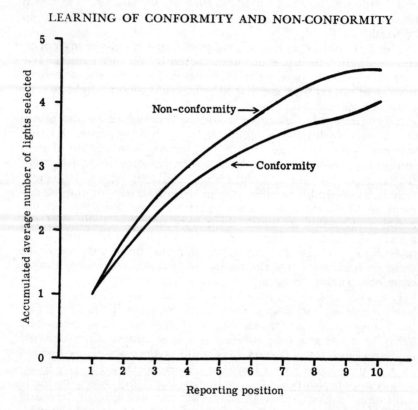

The answer may be seen in Figure 24 for the first version of the experiment, in which there were five lights on the panel and ten persons in the group. Here is plotted the accumulated average number of lights chosen by the subjects in each of the experimental groups by reporting position. It will be remembered that the first person to report his "guess" had no choice but to choose a light not previously chosen. The second subject, however, may make the same choice as the first subject and thus conform, or he may choose a previously unchosen light and thus not conform. If the subtle manipulation of the reward pattern had an effect, then by the time the second person had made his choice, there should have been more lights already chosen in the Non-Conformity Group than in the Conformity Group. After the third person made his choice, there should have been a still greater number of lights chosen in the Non-Conformity Group than in the Conformity Group. Thus a tendency toward non-conformity would show in Figure 24 as a greater number of lights chosen at each position in this group, or conversely, a smaller number of unchosen lights remaining after each subject had his guess.

As is clear in the figure, the effect appears quite markedly even in the brief span of twenty trials. The systematic effort to reward non-conformity in one group and conformity in the other was remarkably successful.

It can be seen in Figure 24 that the two curves tend to converge toward the end. This convergence is a reflection of the fact that the subjects who reported their "guesses" at the end, in either the ninth or tenth positions, had little choice on many occasions. With five lights and ten people it often occurred that there were no more unchosen lights by the time these subjects were given an opportunity to "guess."

The second version of this experiment was carried out to demonstrate that the conformity and non-conformity behavior produced in the first version could be repeated at will. It was also constructed in such a manner that the last person to report had a free choice. Thus, with eight lights and only seven people in the group, every subject but the first one to report had a choice between an already chosen or a previously unchosen light. The results of the second version may be seen in Figure 25. Not only was the effort to produce conformity and non-conformity behavior without the subject being aware of what was happening successful, but the two curves continue to diverge through all positions.

These experiments seem to demonstrate that groups can be made to appear as "individualists" or "conformists" almost at will through subtle but nevertheless effective differential reward for the two forms of behavior. Furthermore, these effects can be produced without those involved being in any sense aware either of the effort made to control their behavior or of the direction which they are being induced to take.

FIGURE 25

LEARNING OF CONFORMITY AND NON-CONFORMITY

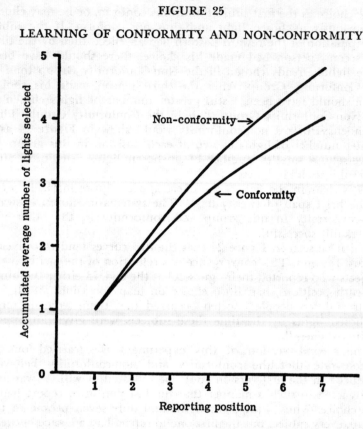

Choice of Betting Odds as an Index of Conformity

Most games offering choices to the player that differ in probability of winning and in the amount of expected return if one does win, offer a built-in possibility of differential reward for conformity or non-conformity. For example, in pari mutuel situations the odds are in direct proportion to the amount of money wagered on each horse. If a large number of people bet on one horse, the odds for that horse will become very small. If there is a horse in the race on which few are willing to wager, then the odds on that horse will be very large or long. Thus, odds in a race are a direct reflection of the number of people who have placed bets on each horse in the race.

Among people who participate in pari mutuel betting the belief exists that some individuals tend to "play the favorites." If this is true, such a person is one who consistently tends to agree with the majority opinion, whatever his stated reasons for doing so. Such a person consistently tends to conform to the social norm or standard reflected in the betting odds. A so-called "long-shot player," assuming there are such people, is one who consistently bets on horses selected by a very small number of people at the track. He may be characterized as a person who consistently tends to be non-conformist with respect to the social norms or standards reflected by the betting odds.

If "playing favorites" can be described as conforming behavior and "playing the long shots" as non-conforming behavior, then a betting situation of this type offers an opportunity to manipulate conformity and non-conformity behavior through the manipulation of differential reward, without the subject being aware that his tendencies to conform or not to conform are in any sense involved in the problem.

Advantage was therefore taken of this covert meaning of choice of odds, and a "horse race game" was invented which could be played in a laboratory setting. The objective of the game for the participant was to win as much money as possible. The objective of the game from an experimental standpoint was to determine if groups of subjects could be made into "conformers" or "non-conformers" in the sense of consistently choosing short or long odds without their being aware that their behavior was being manipulated or that there was anything at all unusual or phony about the pattern of odds in the game.

Forty students from the University of Michigan participated in the game. They came to the laboratory in groups of ten and were told that they were to be subjects in an experiment on betting behavior. It was explained that complete results of two actual racing programs run recently at an Eastern track had been obtained. Since the experiment was about betting behavior with respect to odds alone, all other information from the racing program had been removed—the actual names of horses, jockeys, owners, etc. For the sake of realism, fictitious names were given for each horse. Each person in the group was given the two complete programs, totalling sixteen races, with the information relevant to each race on a single page. Each was also given thirty-two dollars in stage money and instructed that he was to bet two dollars on each race and try to win as much as possible. It was explained that we already knew, of course, which horse had actually won each race. However, each person was to choose which horse he wanted to place a bet on, mark it on his program, and give the "bookie" two dollars. Then the show of a simulated race was presented. The winners were announced, and the "bookie" went around paying off the winners.

The participants in this experiment were enthusiastic and seemed to be enjoying themselves thoroughly. They took the problem of trying to guess the winner quite seriously in a noisy and joking atmosphere. The calling of the race was accompanied by rooting and apprehension. Announcement of the winner was accompanied by groans and whoops. There can be little doubt that the participants were having a wonderful time.

A sample program taken from the game is in Table 5. Each group of ten people was arbitrarily chosen to be a short-priced or

TABLE 5

SAMPLE PROGRAM SHEET FOR THE HORSE RACE GAME

Race no. 2

Horse	Odds
1	3-1
2	5-2
3	5-1
4	6-1
5	8-1
6	6-1
7	8-1
8	12-1
9	12-1
10	15-1
11	15-1
12	8-1

Conformity Group or a long-priced or Non-Conformity Group. The two groups were treated exactly alike and used the same program sheets, but different winners were announced in the two groups. An effort was made to make the odds on each program as realistic as possible. This was accomplished by making the programs very similar to the results of actual races. Races were selected for this purpose, however, from the middle ranges of odds distributions.

There were no races on the programs with extremely long or extremely short odds. The longest odds on any horse in the programs was 30-1, and the shortest price quoted was 6-5.

Choice of the odds to be paid off in the two groups was made to favor short-price winners in the Conformity Group and long-price winners in the Non-Conformity Group. However, while it was necessary to have the difference in odds paid be sufficiently large to produce the desired effect on choices, it was also desirable to keep the difference in treatment between the two groups small enough so that no one would be able to notice anything unusual about the odds on the winners. The actual procedure was to choose winning odds from race programs published in newspapers. The Conformity Group was paid off with odds typical of a normal "favorite's day" and the Non-Conformity Group was paid off with winning odds characteristic of a normal "long-shot player's day." Table 6 shows the odds of the announced winners in the two groups in this experiment, along with the average odds paid in each kind of group over the sixteen-race program. It may seem that a few "long shots" were

TABLE 6

AVERAGE WINNING ODDS IN CONFORMITY

AND NON-CONFORMITY GROUPS

Race	Conformity odds	Non-conformity odds
1	4-1	20-1
2	5-2	12-1
3	3-1	5-1
4	10-1	30-1
5	2-1	2-1
6	3-1	15-1
7	3-1	6-1
8	3-1	4-1
9	3-1	10-1
10	5-2	5-2
11	6-1	8-1
12	2-1	15-1
13	20-1	20-1
14	8-5	10-1
15	3-1	3-1
16	4-1	30-1
Average odds	3.9-1	12.4-1

permitted to win in the Conformity Group and a few favorites were permitted to win in the Non-Conformity Group. None of the sub-

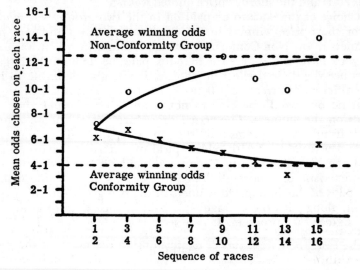

FIGURE 26

LEARNING OF CONFORMITY AND NON-CONFORMITY

jects in this experiment thought the odds on winners were rigged in any way or were in any way unusual or atypical.[3]

The effect of this very modest manipulation of odds paid the winners in the two groups is clear in Figure 26. With no awareness that anything was being done to them, the two groups diverged promptly and widely in their betting behavior. The Conformity Group chose progressively short-priced horses. The Non-Conformity Group increased the length of the odds in its choices by a considerable margin. In fact the behavior of each group appears to be quite sensitive to and responsive to what happened to it. Each group appears to have selected odds very close to the average odds paid during the preceding races.

To the extent to which "playing the favorites" can be described as conforming behavior and "playing the long shots" as non-conforming behavior, the horse race game experiment demonstrates that control of conforming and non-conforming behavior is remarkably easy through differential reward for the two forms of behavior.

Generalization of conformity habits

Habits may be quite specific to a situation or they may be broad and general. A tendency to do what the group does may apply only to a given situation. A student may find studying when others are studying an efficient plan for himself, since it is likely to be quiet when everyone is studying. Thus he may conform to the pattern of behavior of the group in this specific situation. This habit of conforming to the pattern of behavior of the group may not be extended to other situations in which the reasonableness of the behavior is not so apparent. The same student who chooses to conform and study when the others study may choose not to conform in respect to dating, for example. While all the others in his group are dating only seniors because that is the social custom at the moment, he may be dating a sophomore because he likes her company. If so, conformity for him is a specific habit rather than a general one. On the other hand, it is possible that a general habit of conforming or not conforming could be developed on the basis of relative rewards for the two kinds of behavior. A student who finds it rewarding to study when the others study may tend to look to the group for guidance in matters other than the proper time for study. He may systematically begin to behave in accordance with the way other people are behaving in a new situation. If this is the case, then the habit of conforming to the norm of the group as exhibited by its behavior, will have generalized and become a general habit.

The students who participated in these experiments did not differ in their tendencies to conform or not to conform, as groups, before the beginning of the experimental sessions. At the end of each experiment they did. One group was showing conformity behavior and the other non-conformity behavior in the specific situations which had been devised to manipulate and measure the behavior. It is an interesting question whether this minimum kind of influence on the pattern of their behaviors had any lasting quality or any tendency to generalize or carry over to other situations.

A limited kind of test of this proposition was attempted. A series of questions was devised, each of which permitted some kind of analysis in terms of agreement with a group norm or disagreement with it, and these questions were answered by the subjects after the experiment proper was over. The forty subjects who participated in the first extrasensory perception experiment also served as subjects in the horse race game. They were asked four questions shortly after the horse race game was concluded. The forty-two subjects in the second extra-sensory perception experiment were asked seven such questions immediately after the experiment, and twenty-six of these subjects were asked the same seven questions three weeks later.

Some of the questions yielded two independent measures of conformity or non-conformity behavior. Twenty-three tests could be made of any tendency to conform or not to conform which may have generalized or carried over as a residual effect of the "training" to conform or not to conform in a specific situation.

The list of questions and the manner in which conformity or non-conformity behavior could be shown on each one is as follows:

Question 1

As an advertising stunt a clothing store is selling chances for a quarter each. You can buy a chance in any one of five pools which differ in what chance you have of winning and also in how many new clothes you can buy if you win. If you were to buy one chance, which category or pool would you spend your quarter on? The one most frequently chosen so far is the $12.50 category.

Chance of winning	Amount of certificate for clothes for the winners
1 in 10	$ 2.50
1 in 20	5.00
1 in 50	12.50
1 in 100	25.00
1 in 500	125.00

This question permits two different conformity scores. A member of the Conformity Group should tend to choose the greater chance of winning a smaller amount of money, while a member of the Non-Conformity Group should tend to choose the smaller chance of winning a greater amount—simply because so far he has been differentially rewarded for doing or not doing what others do. Thus, a second expectation would be that more members of the Conformity Group would choose the $12.50 category in accordance with the announced norm.

Question 2

This is a question concerning aesthetic preference. Pick out the one figure you think is most stimulating and exciting. Draw a circle around that one. Here I can give you the order of preference of groups which have made this judgment so far. They have chosen them in the order 3, 1, 4, 2, 5. That is, most people have voted for 3, next most for 1, next for 4, next for 2 and least for 5.

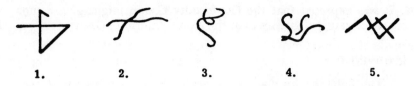

1.   2.   3.   4.   5.

A tendency to conform could be expected to reveal itself by a greater frequency of choice of figure number 3. Non-conformity would be revealed by a greater tendency to choose figure number 5.[4]

Question 3

How many molecules of H_2O are there in a spoonful of water? The only hint I can give you is that the mean of the guesses we have so far is 2,701,000,000.

A tendency to conform should produce guesses grouped closely around the norm of 2,701,000,000, while a tendency not to conform should produce guesses somewhat more deviant than those produced by the Conformity Group.

Question 4

With the development of rockets and guided missiles, many people have come to the conclusion that a trip to the moon by people is not as fantastic as it once sounded. We want you to make a guess as to the year in which you think the first trip to the moon will be accomplished. The mean of the guesses we have had so far is 1993.[5]

Again it would be expected that conformity would manifest itself by guesses close to the announced norm and non-conformity would be shown by more deviant answers.

Question 5

The subjects were shown a piece of cardboard containing a large number of dots, enough, in fact, that a person could make only the haziest kind of guess as to the number of dots on the card. They were then asked:

How many dots are there on this cardboard?

It was expected that the Conformity Group might give a more restricted range of guesses than the Non-Conformity Group.

Question 6

The following lines are variations of an illusion known as the Muller-Lyer illusion. One of the lines is physically longer than the other seven which are of equal length. Which one is the longer line? Number 3 is the most frequently chosen line so far.

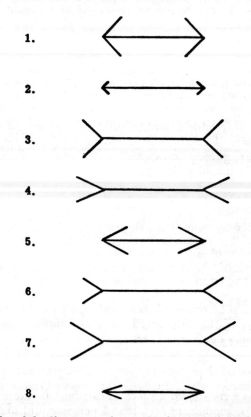

Each of the eight lines are of exactly the same length. Conformity should be revealed by a tendency to choose line number 3, while non-conformity would be shown by an avoidance of a choice of line number 3.

Question 7

You are introduced to a lottery in which the prizes, and the price of each ticket, will be determined at the drawing. The prices of the tickets will range from 25¢ to $2.00, the prizes from $2,000 to $20,000. You are allowed to purchase 8 tickets. How many would you buy? Most people have decided to buy 4.

The Conformity Group should show a greater frequency of choice of four tickets. Non-conformity subjects should choose other numbers of tickets.

Question 8

In horse racing the odds on a horse are determined by the number of people betting on that horse. If the odds on a particular horse are great, few people have selected it to win. On the other hand, if the odds on the horse are small, it has been favored by many at the betting window. If you had been asked to advise a bettor in this race, and if you had no other information, which horse would you have selected? Give me the number of the horse.

HORSE	ODDS
1. HAL PRINCE	9-1
2. MIRA SADOR	3-1
3. SINKIANG	5-1
4. OH DEAR	5-1
5. AQUACATE	3-1
6. EXTRA INNING	10-1
7. GRACIOUS LADY	8-1
8. UGOBY	10-1
9. CHALLESTAR	10-1
10. DIXIE TALK	4-1
11. MARBLE ANN	15-1
12. JOANNE LEE	30-1

It was expected that the Conformity Group would tend to choose short-priced horses, while the Non-Conformity Group would tend to choose long-priced horses even though some of the groups having this question did not participate in the "horse race game."

The answers given to each of these questions can be scored as to whether the Conformity Group had tended to generalize the acquired tendency to conform in comparison with the Non-Conformity Group. The differences in the ways in which the two classes of subjects answered each question tended to be quite small. However, the results on each question on each administration could be scored as to whether the differences between the two groups were in the direction expected from the hypothesis. The results may be seen in Table 7. Of the twenty-three tests eighteen showed differ-

TABLE 7

TESTS OF GENERALIZATION OF

CONFORMITY AND NON-CONFORMITY

Direction of difference	Frequency
In predicted direction	18
No difference	2
Opposite predicted direction	3

ences in the performance of the two classes of subject in the expected direction. It can therefore be concluded that a minimal tendency to conform or not to conform did in fact carry over from these simple experiments to answers to sets of ambiguous questions. There was a small tendency for conformity and non-conformity to act as if they were generalized habits.

Summary

These studies seem to permit a positive conclusion. *Conformity and non-conformity behavior can be manipulated rather easily through the use of differential reward for the two classes of behavior without the person involved being aware that his behavior is being influenced or being aware of the character of the change. Furthermore, even this modest change in the tendency to conform or not to conform tends to generalize and carry over to situations other than the one in which the influence has been exerted.*

Notes for Chapter 7

These studies were carried out by Robert Birney, Harry Burdick, John Caylor, Patricia O'Connor, Alfred Raphelson, and John Swets. William Dember served as the "sender" in the ESP experiments.

[1] Norman R. F. Maier. *Frustration.* (New York: McGraw-Hill Book Company, Inc., 1949.)

[2] This procedure raises a technical difficulty in the distribution of "reward." So that differences between the performances of Conformity and Non-Con-

formity Groups could not be attributed to differences in frequency of reward, the experimenter in the small hidden room had the task of attempting to choose lights in such a manner that the number of subjects rewarded throughout the experiment was the same in a Conformity Group as in a Non-Conformity Group. This could be accomplished only by lighting different numbers of lights in the two groups—more lights in a Non-Conformity Group than in a Conformity Group. Furthermore, he could only approximate such a result since there was insufficient time to maintain a running, trial-by-trial mean number of subjects rewarded.

Despite the difficulty of the task, the experimenter succeeded in producing a very close approximation of equal frequencies of reward in the two types of groups. In the first version the mean numbers of subjects rewarded were 4.7 and 4.35 in the Conformity and Non-Conformity Groups respectively. In the second version the mean numbers were 3.62 and 3.67. In order to accomplish this, he turned on an average of 1.5 and 2.8 lights in the first version and 1.58 and 3.03 lights in the second version of the experiment.

[3] Since the subjects were permitted to bet on any horse they pleased, little control could be exerted over the number of people who won or the amount of money involved. It happened by chance that by the eleventh race the amount of money paid out in the two groups was almost identical, even though there were about three times as many winners in the Conformity Group. By the end of the experiment, however, there had been exactly twice as many winners in the Conformity Group, but the Non-Conformity Group had won nearly three times as much play money.

[4] In the second version of this question three more nonsense figures were added and the statement of order of preference for groups which had made this judgment so far was extended to cover all eight figures.

[5] This study was the first to be carried out in the project. It was done in the Spring of 1952. The estimate of 1993 would have to be revised should such a question be used as a measure of conformity at the present date.

8

AN ANATOMY

FOR CONFORMITY

Conformity behavior was defined in Chapter 1 as movement from one's own position toward a group norm or standard of behavior. Conformity has occurred when a person's attitude or way of behaving is modified or changed through social pressure toward an opinion or mode of acting which is perceived as being more acceptable to others. Non-conformity has occurred when an individual reacts negatively, for whatever reason, to the standards or mores of others. It is not enough to say that the behavior of such a person is deviant from the social norm. The mark of non-conformity is an active rebellion, an overt rejection of social goals.

A basic way of structuring a situation so that conformity and non-conformity behavior may be understood or controlled, is shown in the formula mentioned at the beginning of this study:

$$\text{NEED} \longrightarrow \text{INSTRUMENTAL ACT} \longrightarrow \text{GOAL}$$

This simple formula does not indicate what happens—only how. Any need, any instrumental act, and any goal appropriate to the need may be substituted into its frame. The choice of conformity and non-conformity behavior as instrumental acts is completely arbitrary. This is a simple anatomy for conformity.

Conformity behavior as controlled by the nature of the situation and as a personality trait

In each of the experiments reported in this volume, the amount or frequency of conformity or non-conformity behavior was manipulated through the control of various aspects of the situation in which the subjects found themselves. These findings are in the social science tradition of analysis of effective relationships which appear to be independent of the particular individuals involved. If the amount of conformity in a group can be controlled through the application of social pressure, then it does not matter who the individual group members are or what differences there are among them as individuals.

In several of the studies, efforts were also made to predict who would conform and who would not conform on the basis of measurements of variables showing a wide range of individual differences. For example, in the study of attitudes toward cheating on an examination, conformity behavior was predicted on the basis of individual differences in the ambiguity of a situation. Individual difference predictions were also made in the study of needs in conflict, in which strengths of need for achievement and need for affiliation were used to predict who would continue to work as hard as possible to win in her own group and who would slow down to permit her partner to achieve a measure of success.

The attempt to predict who would and who would not conform from measures of individual differences is in the tradition of the psychology of personality. Here the effort is to ascertain characteristic modes of behavior which occur in a wide variety of situations and thus, to the extent to which they can be described as transsituational, can be designated as personality traits. For example, conformity behavior has been described as a basic mode of behavior, a drive to escape isolation and to achieve a state of belonging. Individuals may differ in the strength and pervasiveness of such a drive and can be described as being more or less conformist.

Conformism as a personality trait has also been asserted to be related to early child-rearing practices. A child with authoritarian parents or with frequent and meaningful contact with other authority figures is likely to develop a personality which can be described as conformist. From this point of view conformity is a generalized habit, is a personality trait, is trans-situational, may be a characteristic of a culture, can be a nearly immutable characteristic of an individual or a population.

It should be clear that the studies reported in the preceding six chapters originated in a philosophy of attempting, wherever possible, to invent a laboratory situation in which the behavior of the group could be manipulated and controlled through the manipulation of the situation, and at the same time to make individual difference predictions in the tradition of personality psychology.

Neither a single experiment nor the whole program of research was designed to obtain an evaluation of the relative contribution of the two kinds of determinants of conformity and non-conformity, but in the course of more than three years of effort a conviction grew that situational determination of conformity was the more powerful approach.

As experiment followed experiment it became readily apparent that almost any operation that could be considered applicable to a group, which might also be expected to modify the degree of conformity, was likely to be effective. It clearly would have been quite easy to produce universal conformity or non-conformity in the groups. The real problem was one of how to balance the factors in such a way that some subjects would conform and some would not. This was necessary, of course, if predictions were to be made from any of the measures of individual differences. The problem was to prevent situational factors from simply overwhelming any other possible determinant.

That the amount of manifest conformity in young adults could be modified in the laboratory, and in such a short time (Chapter 7), is an argument for the point that if these subjects possessed personality traits of conformity and non-conformity, these traits must have been labile in the extreme, rather than rigid and inflexible as would be expected from the usual conception of personality traits. To be significant social factors, such tendencies should be deep-seated and not subject to easy modification by petty and insignificant experiences like a horse race game in the laboratory.

Finally, from the standpoint of efforts to produce desirable social change, situational manipulation offers hope of change *here and now*. The conception of conformity as a personality trait would require that a present state be endured for a minimum of a generation while changes in child-rearing practice have had sufficient time to become effective.

The role of laboratory experimentation

The past six chapters contain reports of many laboratory experiments, each of which has been devised to demonstrate one or more functional relationships between discernible variables, such as stimulus ambiguity, and conformity and non-conformity behavior. The reader may ask why the time, effort, and money were devoted to laboratory demonstrations when the perspective of hindsight leaves little doubt that each of the factors which have been investigated do in fact operate in the control of conformity and non-conformity as well as other forms of behavior. He may ask whether similar conclusions might have been reached without spending the time and enduring the trouble necessary to invent and carry out experimental demonstrations.

The answer lies in the degree of confidence one may place in conclusions reached on the basis of experiment compared with conclusions reached on the basis of *naturalistic observation*. Naturalistic observation is the beginning point and basis for almost all theory, explanation, and experimentation. It consists of careful, objective, systematic observation. It constitutes the source of a variety of hypotheses or tentative explanations of the variables which may be related to the observed phenomena. The choice between alternate explanations is a matter of debate, discussion, reason, and a weighing of complex evidence. Experimentation often consists in an effort to test the adequacy of the conclusions which have been reached on the basis of naturalistic observation and logical analysis. Experiments of the type reported in this volume are for the most part efforts to clarify, to quantify, and to increase the certainty of statements of relations. If a variable can be shown to be functionally related to the behavior in question in the laboratory, then one has greater confidence that the relationship is likely to hold in real-life situations.

Each experimental study or group of studies has resulted in a conclusion or proposition concerning a relationship that can be expected to control the character of the behavior under normal circumstances. Each proposition also offers a technique of deliberate manipulative control of behavior for good or evil. Just as each original proposition constituted an hypothesis to be tested in an experiment, once the validity of the proposition was demonstrated, it could be taken as a general principle useful in explaining the determinants of ordinary behavior. The remainder of this chapter is an effort to indicate how each of the propositions, now experimentally demonstrated, can be broadened, and the extent to which they can be fit into an over-all blueprint for the situational manipulation of conformity behavior.

Résumé

The relatively restricted conclusions drawn from the results of the experiments may be restated in a more general form to constitute a blueprint for conformity. Both the particular experimental conclusions and the broader generalizations may be stated under the following headings: Needs and Conformity, Need———→Instrumental Act Relations, Instrumental Acts, Instrumental Act———→ Goal Relations, and Goals.

Needs and conformity

It should be obvious without the need for experimental demonstration that *the stronger the need which can only be served by conformity behavior, the greater will be the tendency to conform.*
One may ask whether conformity as a class of behavior is uniquely served by any particular human motive. There is no easy answer to such a question. Although motivation theory is quite complex, the requirements for the identification of a theoretically useful motive are simple. It is only necessary to identify a class of arousal conditions which produce persistent activity until an appropriate and identifiable goal is reached.
A part of the rationale underlying some of the experiments reported here was that there might be a close association between conformity behavior and need for Affiliation. The norm or standard is inextricably related to a social group of some description. Need for Affiliation is a basic social need satisfied by the establish-

ment, maintenance, or enhancement of a warm interpersonal relationship. It encompasses the desire for approval of or acceptance by others. It should be noted, however, that in the study of needs in conflict, it was the relation with a single friend which was at stake in the experimental demonstration. Whether need for Affiliation is clearly relevant to acceptance by a larger, impersonal group was not tested. Thus the need for Affiliation is clearly a theoretically useful human motive by the above definition, but a unique relationship to conformity has not been established.

On the other hand, it is clear that while need for Affiliation might be a relevant need in the production of conformity behavior in many social situations, it is only one of hundreds of human needs which might have been chosen to serve the purpose. Conformity can be induced by making it a prerequisite for the satisfaction of hunger on the one hand, or the most abstract of human needs on the other. Therefore, any special relationship between need for Affiliation and conformity would certainly be no more than one of relative frequency of association in everyday social life. Such an association could be established only through a major survey research effort.

Conformity and Need——→Instrumental Act Relations

As a result of the study of conformity and the conflict of needs, the conclusion was drawn that *in a situation where conformity is instrumental to the satisfaction of one need and non-conformity is instrumental to the satisfaction of another, the behavior that will occur depends on the relative strengths of the two needs.*

Rarely, however, does an individual face a situation in which the range of needs or the range of instrumental acts or ways of behaving are so simple and dichotomous. It is much more frequently the case that a large variety of human needs are present, a wide range of behaviors available, and the determination of which one will occur is an exceedingly complex function. There is little doubt, however, that selection of an instrumental act can be determined by the relative strengths of the needs present.

When conformity to some social group norm or standard is one of a variety of available ways of behaving, conformity will occur when, other things being equal, it appears to serve a complex of functional human needs greater in sum than that served by any other available instrumental act.

Conformity and the instrumental act

Conformity behavior is an instrumental act—movement from one's own position or attitude or way of behaving to one which is closer to that specified by a social norm or standard. The elements of the situation which can be varied are the aspects of the individual's own position, the pattern of movement or behavior change open to the person, and the characteristics of the norm toward which social pressure is applied.

Clarity and value of the person's own position. Experimental demonstrations yielded two closely related conclusions relevant to aspects of the person's own position as they affected the amount of conformity to be expected from social pressure applied toward a norm. They are the following: *The more familiar the subject is with the target of the attitude or behavior to be influenced by the norm, the less effective the pressure toward conformity or nonconformity. Susceptibility to social pressure will vary with the degree of certainty the subject has in his own solution to the problem.*

While these conclusions were derived from a highly artificial study of attitudes toward impersonal groups and from a highly abstract problem-solving situation, they constitute specific manifestations of a highly general and important functional aspect of conformity behavior. The larger the amount and the better the quality of the information possessed by a person about an object of attitudes or behavior, the more intimate and personal the association, the less effective will be social pressure toward conformity. In short, *the better the education, the more independent and self-determined the behavior, the less the conformity under social pressure.*

Relative clarity or ambiguity of what behavior constitutes conformity. The experiment on the relation of stimulus ambiguity and conformity led to this conclusion: *Conformity behavior can be expected to vary with the degree of stimulus ambiguity in a social situation as seen by a given person or as determined by the nature of the situation itself. If he sees the situation as one in which alternate behaviors open to him are few in number and well-defined, social pressure is unlikely to produce much change in his attitudes or behavior. If he sees the situation as permitting many alternate behaviors, and if he is uncertain about the degree of appropriateness of the alternates, social pressure can be expected to produce considerable conformity.*

This conclusion, as drawn from the experiment, is in a very general form. Conformity can be produced in highly ambiguous situations simply because the person involved has no idea what to do or how to do it and is thus more open to the effects of social pressure than he would be if the alternate courses of action and their implications were clear to him. Thus, *the more ambiguous the situation, the more vague and numerous the alternate courses of action open to a person, the more the conformity in response to social pressure.*

Relative clarity, value, and remoteness of the norm. Three conclusions emerge from the experiments relative to various aspects of the norm toward which movement was induced by the application of social pressure: *The effectiveness of a given norm can be enhanced or reduced by attributing high or low value to it. The more the norm agrees with the subject's own experience, the more effective it is likely to be. Conversely, the greater the discrepancy between the norm and what the subject thinks is right, the less effective will be the pressure. The greater the disagreement between the norm and another source of information designated as "official" or "correct," the less effective will be the norm in modifying the subject's behavior.*

Pressure toward the adoption of an attitude or way of behaving can clearly be made more or less effective depending upon the value or importance attributed to the behavior. The relation between conformity behavior and the size of the gap between the person's behavior and the behavior toward which social pressure is applied is not so obvious. It is reasonably clear that if the difference is small, pressure should be effective. It was not established in the studies reported in this volume, but there is some indication that not only does the effectiveness of social pressure decrease as the gap or amount of required change grows greater, but there is a distance beyond which social pressure is likely to have a reverse effect. That is, if the discrepancy between the person's behavior and that demanded by social pressure is extreme, the effect of the application of pressure toward conformity may be to produce even greater nonconformity. In any case, what evidence there is permits the conclusion that the less the gap the more certain the effectiveness of social pressure.

The third conclusion derives from the application of the dimension of stimulus ambiguity to the norm. The effect is the reverse of that seen in the application of the concept of stimulus ambiguity to the mode of behavior. If "official" or "correct" information is offered in conflict with the norm, the effect is to create ambiguity concerning the norm itself. The effect of such ambiguity is to reduce its effectiveness. Conflict or disagreement between "official" information and a norm may also be viewed as a manipulation of the norm value. To the extent that "official" or "correct" information has value as a rational solution, offering it detracts from the perceived value of the social group norm with which it conflicts.

The three experimental conclusions can be reformulated into a simple statement about aspects of the norm and their effects on conformity: *The clearer the norm, the higher its attributed value, and the closer it is to a person's own position, the more effective it will be in producing conformity behavior.*

Conformity and Instrumental Act———→Goal Relations

Experiments reported here demonstrated the relative validity of the following conclusion: *If conformity is seen as instrumental to being liked or accepted, the amount of conformity will vary as a function of the relative attractiveness of the group and thus the degree of satisfaction or security attached to being accepted by the group. However, if conformity is not seen as being instrumental to being liked, then effective group pressure toward conformity is likely to produce rejection of the group and non-conformity.*

Consequently, group pressure is not enough. For it to be effective in producing conformity, the person involved must see the behavior in question as the only way to achieve the goal and must feel certain that this avenue really leads to realization of the goal. Otherwise, a degree of conformity may be produced by social pressure in the particular situation in which it is applied; but the net effect may be for the person to resent the manipulation, to feel that conformity will not be effective in achieving his acceptance by the group, reject the group, and then find ways to avoid the pressure. Finally, the net effect may be non-conformity as an active process in subsequent situations. Thus the general conclusion is reached that *for social pressure to be effective in producing conformity, the person must see conformity as an effective avenue to achieving the goal of acceptance by the group.*

Conformity and the goal

The limited or restricted experimental conclusions reached about aspects of the goals to be made relevant to conformity are these:

*The more familiar the subject is with the reference group to which
the norm is attributed, the more effective will be the norm in producing conformity. Conformity and non-conformity behavior can
be manipulated rather easily through the use of differential reward
for the two classes of behavior without the person's awareness of
the influence on his behavior or of the character of the change.
Furthermore, even this modest change in a tendency to conform or
not to conform tends to generalize and carry over to situations
other than the one in which the influence was exerted.*

These conclusions contain several basic ideas. The more intimate
the association between the person and the group to which the
norm is attributed, the greater the power of the group to reward
the person by expressions of approval and acceptance. While intimacy of association may certainly encompass many other relationships, some of which may well have an influence on the effectiveness
of the group in producing conformity, the power to reward is certainly an important one. Thus a manifestation of acceptance by the
group is a larger reward the more intimate the association. This
limited conclusion relates to a very broad principle of behavior
theory: that the larger a reward, the more effective it will be in producing a certain behavior and in establishing the behavior as an
habitual mode of response. Besides, intimacy of association also
implies frequency of association. Therefore, close association provides a greater opportunity first for frequent rewards and then for
the operation of the well-known positive relationship between the
number of rewards and the strength of the habit. Thus, intimacy
of association provides the conditions for the operation of the
powerful principles relating size and frequency of reward to the
control of behavior.

The particular conclusions also involve a limited version of the
principle that broad and generalized ways of behaving may be controlled by reward. Conformity, the tendency to change one's way
of thinking or behaving to correspond more closely with the behavior of the group, is just such a generalized way of meeting a wide
variety of specific situations. In the experiments where conformity
and non-conformity were manipulated through the repeated application of reward, the specific response which was rewarded was
never that of conforming or not conforming. These general tendencies emerged only through a reward contingency which was a
characteristic of the whole series of responses rather than of any
one response. Thus conformity and non-conformity were trans-

situational, both in the original experiments and in the subsequent demonstration of generalization to other situations or other kinds of responses.

Finally, it is important that conformity and non-conformity were manipulated in these studies without the knowledge of the subjects, and certainly without their being aware that their success or lack of success was in any way related to what the majority of the group chose to do.

A somewhat more general conclusion may then be stated: *The greater and more valued the reward, the oftener it is achieved through conformity behavior, the more conformist the behavior is likely to become, and the more likely it is to become a generalized way of behaving in new situations. The person need not be aware of these effects.*

How to Do It

If one wishes to produce conformity for good or evil, the formula is clear. Manage to arouse a need or needs that are important to the individual or to the group. Offer a goal which is appropriate to the need or needs. Make sure that conformity is instrumental to the achievement of the goal and that the goal is as large and as certain as possible. Apply the goal or reward at every opportunity. Try to prevent the object of your efforts from obtaining an uncontrolled education. Choose a setting that is ambiguous. Do everything possible to see that the individual has little or no confidence in his own position. Do everything possible to make the norm which you set appear highly valued and attractive. Set it at a level not too far initially from the starting position of the individual or the group and move it gradually toward the behavior you wish to produce. Be absolutely certain you know what you want and that you are willing to pay an enormous price in human quality, for whether the individual or the group is aware of it or not, the result will be CONFORMITY.

INDEX